Maria W. Miller Stewart

Meditations From the Pen of Mrs. Maria W. Stewart

Now Matron of the Freedmen's Hospital, and Presented in 1832 to the

First African Baptist Church and Society of Boston, Mass.

Maria W. Miller Stewart

Meditations From the Pen of Mrs. Maria W. Stewart
Now Matron of the Freedmen's Hospital, and Presented in 1832 to the First African Baptist Church and Society of Boston, Mass.

ISBN/EAN: 9783337125349

Printed in Europe, USA, Canada, Australia, Japan

Cover: Foto ©Lupo / pixelio.de

More available books at **www.hansebooks.com**

MEDITATIONS

FROM THE PEN OF

MRS. MARIA W. STEWART,

(WIDOW OF THE LATE JAMES W. STEWART,)

NOW MATRON OF THE FREEDMAN'S HOSPITAL,

AND

*Presented in 1832 to the First African
Baptist Church and Society of
Boston, Mass.*

FIRST PUBLISHED BY W. LLOYD GARRISON & KNAP.

---

*Now most respectfully Dedicated to the Church Militant
of Washington, D. C.*

WASHINGTON:
ENTERPRISE PUBLISHING COMPANY,
1879.

ERRATA.

•**PAGE** 10—Third paragraph, first line, read "this" instead of "the."

PAGE 36—Omit "black" before "book," in tenth line; second line from bottom, substitute "fearful" for "faithful."

PAGE 37—First line, prefix "un" before fashionable."

PAGE 40—In fifth line of the prayer insert "though" after "but."

PAGE 41—Meditation VI., line 39 – Read "nor the horrors of hell."

PAGE 42—Insert "my" after "O," third paragraph.

PAGE 47—Substitute "ascended" for "extended," fourteenth line.

PAGE 63—Substitute "our" for "the," before "greatest," first line.

PAGE 66—Insert "so" after "been," tenth line.

PAGE 71—"Methinks instead of "bethinks" fourth line.

PAGE 81—Insert "in" after "that," first line.

PREFACE.

—.o.—

The Christian public will undoubtedly be astonished at the humble source from which this work emanates. Nevertheless it must be a God-send, as every one must be convinced who may read its pages. The work was suppressed for forty-six years; and the author was struggling during that time in widowhood and sorrow to maintain her dignity and standing as a woman and a Christian in poverty's dark shade. The work has come up through the wonderful development of the knowledge that she had a claim in the United States Navy Department, for services rendered by her late husband to the Government in the war of 1812. To establish her claim she procured all her evidence from Boston. The author believes that God's time has come for the work to be recognized among His people; for God seeth not as man seeth, but uses such instruments as He sees proper to bring about His most wise and glorious purposes. That God's blessing may accompany the work, and that souls may be brought to the knowledge of the truth as it is in Jesus, is the prayer of the unworthy author.

Feeling a deep solemnity of soul, in view of our wretched and degraded situation, and sensible of the gross ignorance that prevails among us, I have thought proper thus publicly to express my sentiments before you. I hope my friends will not scrutinize these pages with too severe an eye, as I have not calculated to display either elegance or taste in their composition, but have merely written the meditations of my heart as far as my imagination led; and have presented them before you, in order to arouse you to exertion, and to enforce upon your minds the great necessity of turning your attention to knowledge and improvement:

I was born in Hartford, Connecticut, in 1803; was left an orphan at five years of age; was bound out in a clergyman's family; had the seeds of piety and virtue early sown in my mind, but was deprived of the advantages of education, though my soul thirsted for knowledge. Left them at fifteen years of age; attended Sabbath schools until I was twenty; in 1826 was married to James W. Stewart; was left a widow in 1829; was, as I humbly hope and trust, brought to the knowledge of the truth, as it is in Jesus, in 1830; in 1831 made a public profession of my faith in Christ.

From the moment I experienced the change I felt a strong desire, with the help and assistance of God, to devote the remainder of my days to piety and virtue, and now possess that spirit of independence that, were I called upon, I would willingly sacrifice my life for the cause of God and my brethren.

All the nations of the earth are crying out for liberty and equality. Away, away with tyranny and oppression! And shall Afric's sons be silent any longer? Far be it from me to recommend to you either to kill, burn, or destroy. But I would strongly recommend to you to improve your talents; let not one lie buried in the earth. Show forth your powers of mind, Prove to the world that

Though black your skins as shades of night,
Your hearts are pure, your souls are white.

M. W. STEWART.

LETTERS AND COMMENDATIONS.

WASHINGTON CITY, D. C., *July*, 1879.

Truth is sometimes more strange that fiction, as is most happily illustrated in the remarkable case of Mrs. Maria W. Stewart, the worthy widow of the late James W. Stewart, who did efficient service in the Navy of the United States during the war of 1812. Mrs. Stewart, after an honorable widowhood of nearly fifty years, during which time she has sustained herself by patient, persevering industry, in spite of many adverse circumstances, has now gained a limited competency. For some time past her usefulness has been manifested at the Freedman's Hospital in this District. Last fall Dr. G. S. Palmer, M. D., surgeon in charge of the hospital, gave Mrs. Stewart a letter of introduction to the subscriber, with a request to have an examination made of Mrs. Stewart's claim for pension. The facts and circumstances in her favor at first appeared to be " few and far between ;" but by the aid of her retentive memory and by virtue of important documentary and other evidence obtained from Boston and Washington City, D. C., the necessary applications and proof were made to the Pension Office for pension and bounty land ; and in March, 1879, a pension of $8 per month was granted to Mrs. Maria W. Stewart, commencing with March 9, 1878 ; and in due time she will probably be granted a land warrant for one hundred and sixty acres of Government domain. A combination of providential incidents and circumstances seem to have culminated in her favor to bring about such an unexpected and happy result. With prudence and economy the prospects for the "lone widow" are substantially brightened ; and by the material aid thus obtained she hopes to be able soon to produce and republish her little volume of religious thoughts, contemplations, and early reminiscences, much of which is connected with her early, zealous, devout, and happy experience.

AMOS HUNT,
Notary Public, No. 210 *A street N. E.,*
Washington City, D. C.

MRS. MARIA W. STEWART:

DEAR MADAM: It is seldom, indeed, that two persons, after a separation of forty-six years, are permitted to see each other again in the flesh. It was specially gratifying to me, therefore, to have a visit from you to-day, as for a long period I had entirely lost sight of you, and knew not whether you were living or dead. The sight of you at once carried me back in memory to the very commencement of the anti-slavery movement in this city. You had then not long been married, and were in the flush and promise of a ripening womanhood, with a graceful form and a pleasing countenance. Soon after I started the publication of *The Liberator* you made yourself known to me by coming into my office and putting into my hands, for criticism and friendly advice, a manuscript embodying your devotional thoughts and aspirations, and also various essays pertaining to the condition of that class with which you were complexionally identified—a class "peeled, meeted out, and trodden under foot." You will recollect, if not the surprise, at least the satisfaction I expressed on examining what you had written—far more remarkable in those early days than it would be now, when there are so many educated persons of color who are able to write with ability. I not only gave you words of encouragement, but in my printing office put your manuscript into type, an edition of which was struck off, in tract form, subject to your order. I was impressed by your intelligence and excellence of character. That was nearly half a century ago. Through what marvellous experiences and changes we have since passed! How many rights and privileges are now accorded to the colored people at the North that were then everywhere denied them! And, though there is still a good deal of complexional prejudice to contend with, the change for the better is so great as to furnish cause for devout thanksgiving. But the marvel of marvels has been the total abolition of the old slave system at the South, and the transformation of its victims into full citizenship. True, their present condition is a very pitiable one, owing to the malignity of their former owners; nevertheless, as compared with what they were and what they had to endure as chattels personal, it is for them a great deliverance. I feel sure that a just God will yet fully vindicate their cause, and pour his retribution upon their cruel persecutors.

Your whole adult life has been devoted to the noble task of educating and elevating your people, sympathizing with them in their affliction, and assisting them in their needs ; and, though advanced in years, you are still animated with the spirit of your earlier life, and striving to do what in you lies to succor the outcast, reclaim the wanderer, and lift up the fallen. In this blessed work may you be generously assisted by those to whom you may make your charitable appeals, and who may have the means to give efficiency to your efforts.

Cherishing the same respect for you that I had at the beginning, I remain your friend and well-wisher,

WM. LLOYD GARRISON.

BIOGRAPHICAL SKETCH.

About 1867 I became acquainted with the subject of this sketch in the city of Washington, D. C., a lady exceedingly modest and very retiring in her expression. I at once became deeply interested in her, because there was a quiet sadness and melancholy of expression which, to a close observer, denoted a life of sorrow and disappointment. But soon after I lost sight of her, as she obtained a position under the Government, and by her more than faithful attention to her duties she almost entirely excluded herself from the outside world, and I rarely ever met her, excepting she was going or coming from church or Sabbath-school, or from visiting or gathering in the school poor and destitute children in the neighborhood of the hospital, so they might be taught to fear God and keep His Commandments.

In the month of September, 1878, I called at the Freedmen's Hospital to say farewell to the matron—my friend, Mrs. Stewart ; and as a law had recently passed Congress granting pension to the widows of the war of 1812, and her late husband, James W. Stewart, having served four years under Commodores Porter and Decatur, and doing laudable service for the Government, he was honorably discharged in 1815 ; and as Mrs. Stewart (formerly Miss Miller, of Hartford, Conn.,) had married Mr. Stewart in Boston, where they both resided, she was left a widow in three years and four months after marriage. When I told my friend, Mrs. Stewart, I was coming to Boston she requested of me to do her a favor by investigating her case, and to find if there were persons living who might identify her as the widow of James W. Stewart. I of course promised her I would do all I could when I arrived in Boston, and I did so. One of the first things I did was to find some of the oldest citizens of color in the city of Boston, as Mr. Stewart had been dead forty-nine years. I finally succeeded in finding sufficient evidence from four reliable witnesses, who were personally acquainted with both Mr. and Mrs. Stewart. The witness made oath to the above statement. I had the affidavits made out, and sent them to Washington. She presented her claim to the Department, and it was accepted.

In investigating her case I was startled at the developments made, and at once understood why she carried such a sad, sorrowful, and mysterious countenance. In having occasion to very often visit the different courts I found her husband had been a gentleman of wealth, and left her amply provided for; but the executors literally robbed and cheated her out of every cent; so she was left entirely alone in the world—without mother, father, sister, or brother—in fact, not a living relative in the world to care for her, and with so much amiability and piety of character that she would have suffered wrong rather than defend her rights. She knew there was a will made, but never heard it read, as one of the executors took it out of the house as soon as it was drawn up—which was two days previous to her husband's death. She never knew the contents of her husband's will until 1879, when I myself informed her. It was made on the 15th of December, 1829.

In investigating her case I made frequent visits to the different courts, to find her marriage record and also his death record. I heard there was a will made. I also visited the Probate Court. I asked for the will; it was given to me; and I spent quite a time in reading it over, with surprise and indignation. I cannot express the horror I felt at the great wrong and injustice done the poor, helpless woman, now far advanced in years; but at that time one of the most beautiful and loveliest of women. O, what a shame—what a dreadful shame—for those robbers to so shamefully cheat her out of all that her husband had left her, and to send her away penniless, to combat a heartless world, among strangers. But surely God was good to her and *did* answer her prayers, as she devoutly prayed to Him for His guidance and protection, and she now blesses His Holy Name for keeping her through these many long years. Immediately after the death of her husband, she wrote and published her book; then went to New York; went to school seven years; then taught school several years; finally went South and did good work in instructing and teaching her unfortunate race. If it had not been for the pension bill that passed, she might have died in ignorance of the existence of her book, as she had not seen a copy of it for over forty years. In my great search to find evidence to identify her as the widow of the late James W. Stewart, I found out a great many marvelous things that would have remained hidden until the end of time. I also found out, from all the old personal friends of Mrs. Stewart, that she was then, as now, a very devout Christian lady, a leader in all good movements and reforms, and had no equal as a lecturer or authoress in her day; and I have no doubt if she could have had the advantages of an early education and an opportunity to have developed her superior intellect, she would have been the equal, if not the superior, of her sisters of the more favorite race. But, as it is, she is really a remarkable person, considering all under which she has labored; and I hope now, as our Heavenly Father has permitted her to live to see the injustice that has been done to her, she may be spared still many years to enjoy life as she never has before; and when life's journey is ended here, she will then receive her reward, for her work has been well and faithfully done on earth, and her summons will be, "Well done, thou good and faithful one; enter into the Kingdom prepared for you from the foundation."

LOUISE C. HATTON.

BOSTON, May 28, 1879.

I have been requested by Mrs. Maria W. Stewart, the author of this little volume, to make mention to its readers the fact of my acquaintance with and my knowledge of her at the time this book was first published. Forty years or more have passed since that event. I was then a mere boy, returning home from Oneida Institute with Henry H.

1*

(now the Rev. Dr.) Garnett and Thomas Sidney, my fellow students, where we had been some three years under the instruction of that eminent thinker and preacher, Rev. Beriah Green. I remember very distinctly the great surprise of both my friends and myself at finding in New York a young woman of my own people full of literary aspiration and ambitious of authorship. In those days, that is at the commencement of the anti-slavery enterprise, the desire for learning was almost exclusively confined to colored young *men*. There were a few young women in New York who thought of these higher things, and it was a surprise to find another added to their number.

Mrs. Stewart came to New York with less of the advantages of education than this small literary circle, but full of the greed for literature and letters. She was then a young widow, and still very much distressed at the loss of her husband. The anguish that occurrence had brought to her caused the outburst of an overwrought soul in these "Meditations and Prayers," which she had published a year or so before. The surprise of the case was that a person who had received but six weeks' schooling, who could not even pen her own thoughts, who had to get a little girl ten years old to write every word of this book—that *such* a person could compose essays of this kind and give expression to such thoughts and be the author of such a work !

Mrs. Stewart's case excited much interest. She was received with much consideration. Her eagerness for instruction was gladly met by the school teachers of New York, and in the circle of my own acquaintance young women willingly aided her in the study of arithmetic, geography, grammar, and other branches. Ere long she became a member of a "Female Literary Society," and I remember of listening, on more than a few occasions, to some of her compositions and declamations.

From the beginning she advanced to sufficient fitness to become a public school teacher, and served as such in New York and Brooklyn. In 1853 she came South, and has since been engaged in teaching in Baltimore and Washington.

Now in her old days, encouraged thereto by several of her early friends, and especially by WILLIAM LLOYD GARRISON, who was one of her earliest benefactors, Mrs. Stewart has desired to republish these "Meditations." It is a singular fact that only a few months before his death Mr. Garrison was glad to renew his acquaintance with Mrs. Stewart, and very kindly gave her a letter which refers to this volume and the circumstances of its first publication, which were well known to him at that time.

With the hope that this little book may be of service to many souls, and aid as an encouragement to many hopeful and aspiring young spirits among my people, I very gladly commend it to its several readers.

ALEX. CRUMMELL.

I take great pleasure in saying something in behalf of the work done by Mrs. Maria W. Stewart, a woman of great piety and virtue, who came to Washington during the late war, without friends or relatives, to lend a helping hand toward educating her race. She taught Sabbath school for the Church of the Epiphany, under the direction of Rev. Dr. Hall, in the morning, and in the afternoon for the Church of the Incarnation, on Twelfth street, and after this for Trinity Parish, on Ridge street, thus gaining many friends among all classes.

In 1871 she opened a Sunday school near the Freedman's Hospital, under the care of the Episcopal Church. Through the influence of Dr. Reyburn she collected the sum of two hundred ($200) dollars, with which she bought a comfortable building, and since then has managed a Sabbath school of seventy-five scholars. At times she has lacked teachers, but whenever an earnest call was made, students from the Howard University have always offered their services to help on the good cause. Too much cannot be said in praise of this excellent woman. The aim of her life is to promote the glory of God and the welfare of men.

Yours for the cause's sake,

WM. B. JEFFERSON,
Pastor of Third Baptist Church.

I have been requested to state what I know about the work done by Mrs. Maria W. Stewart in behalf of her race in this city during the war and since that time. I became personally acquainted with her in 1863, when she first came to work in our midst. She organized a school and succeeded in interesting the people in the great work of educating their children. I know how hard she labored to establish this school. My own children were among her first scholars. In a short time the people of this District decided to start an independent free school. A meeting was called and a committee, of which I was a member, was appointed. We then persuaded Mrs. Stewart to combine her school with the free school, and to use all of her influence in keeping up a free District school. She labored for a few months in this school. but being an Episcopalian, and this denomination not being favorable to free schools. we concluded to dismiss her unless she would agree to forsake her denomination. This she refused to do, and the result was she was discharged. However, she soon organized a pay school, and many persons like myself preferred to pay for their children's instruction, and thus have them taught by Mrs. Stewart. Through much suffering and great labor she succeeded in building up her private school. I have seen her going through the streets in the dead of winter looking up the little children who should be attending school; and whether their parents could pay or not, she was perfectly willing to give her time and strength in teaching them.

Her work in the District of Columbia among her people has made me consider her a "true teacher in Israel," because after laboring in the school-room all the week she considered it her duty to do something more in the way of education. She made out of her day school a general Sabbath school, that she might teach the children the wisdom of repentance, and also a knowledge of Him "who is the giver of every good and perfect gift."

Mrs. Stewart has done a great work here. Truly can we say of her that she "went about doing good." And she justly merits all the praise which has been bestowed upon her, because she has always highly sustained her dignity, both spiritual and moral, as an earnest and conscientious Christian worker.

Most respectfully,
HENRY BAILEY.
Pastor of Abyssinian Baptist Church.

SUFFERINGS DURING THE WAR.

CHAPTER I.

It was on a beautiful Sunday morning in the month of
——, in the year of ——, between the hours of 10 and
1 o'clock. The bells were ringing; the people were
going to and fro, and the officers were riding the streets
with white scarfs on their arms. News had just reached
Baltimore that the rebels had encamped five miles from
the city. The churches assembled, but were soon dis-
missed. All was commotion. Everybody who could think
of such a thing was on the eve of flying.

"And what are you going to do?" said a young lady
to me.

"O," said I; "I shall go with Mr. and Mrs. ——."

"But they may not want you to go with them," said
the young lady.

"Then I will go with so and so," I replied.

"And perhaps they might not want you to go with
them," replied she sarcastically.

I answered indignantly: "O, God will take care of
me, if He sends an angel to do it!"

And God did take care of me; for an order was passed
that none of the poor people need pay their rent; so the
money I had saved to pay my rent I took and paid my
way to Washington.

Having lost my position in Williamsburg, Long Island,
and hearing the colored people were more religious and
God-fearing in the South, I wended my way to Baltimore
in 1852. But I found all was not gold that glistened;
and when I saw the want of means for the advancement
of the common English branches, with no literary re-
sources for the improvement of the mind scarcely, I
threw myself at the foot of the Cross, resolving to
make the best of a bad bargain; and there I lay;
and then arose, in the strength of the Lord and in the
power of His might, wrote my programme, printed and
issued my circulars, stating I would open school and
would teach reading, writing, spelling, mental and prac-
tical arithmetic, and whatever other studies called for.
Not knowing the prices, I found myself teaching every
branch for 50 cents per month, until informed by another

teacher that no writing was taught for less than $1 per month. Bought wit is the dearest wit. I have never been very shrewd in money matters; and being classed as a lady among my race all my life, and never exposed to any hardship, I did not know how to manage. I had been teaching in New York and Williamsburg, and had the means of always paying my way. But when I came to teach a pay school I found the difference. But God promised that my bread and water should be sure; and having food and raiment I was content. I would make enough just to supply my wants for the time being, but not a dollar over. I did not make any charge for wood and coal. And always had that refined sentiment of delicacy about me that I could not bear to charge for the worth of my labor. If any loss was to be sustained the loss was always on my side, and not on the side of the parent or the scholar. But toward the commencement of the war the times began to be hard, and I began to be poor, and had to resort to exhibitions and festivals to pay my rent; and, getting sick, became discouraged. I went to a colored gentleman (a man of influence) and to a lady friend and stated my contition, telling the amount of rent I owed; and they expressed their sympathy for me in strong terms, and said if I would be willing to have it put on the programme that I was poor, they would get up an entertainment for my benefit. I consented. They got up the festival with the help of others; made $300; gave me $30 to pay my rent; paid expenses, then divided the remainder among themselves, and then laughed ready to kill themselves to think what a fool they had made of me. I never noticed it, but quietly went on and did the best I could. They flourished like the green bay tree for several years, enjoying the good things of this life. But lo! they passed away and their places were no more to be found. They left no sweet-smelling savor around them, no fragrance, no poor to embalm and bless their memory for their

Little acts of kindness
And little deeds of love.

The children of this world are wiser in their generation than the children of light, sayeth the Scripture. I never could get along like some people, and was always struggling to keep my head above water; but I could never get money enough to carry me home, and would not go unless

I could go looking as well in appearance as I did when I came away. Many were the bitter tears I shed to think I had left all my friends at the North and had come here among strangers. Oh! many were the tears I shed! But it was no use to cry for spilt milk; so I went on serving the Lord, turning neither to the right hand nor to the left; always attending church and Sunday school, trying to be useful in some way. It must be that I was kept by the mighty power of God through faith unto salvation, or I never could have surmounted my difficulties. I had brought letters of introduction to the minister of Saint James' Church, and had attended the services of the church regularly, but becoming dissatisfied, left and worshipped at Mount Calvary, and was never treated better in my life during my short stay among them, and was referred from that church to Trinity at Washington; and one of the motives that induced me to come to this city was to seek a habitation for my God to dwell in, not dreaming that I should ever own a house adapted to that purpose.

CHAPTER II.

During the rebellion, just before the candidacy of General McClellan to the Presidency of the United States, the different denominations of Christians issued an edict among themselves that they would establish their own schools and supply their own teachers. It was the general topic of conversation among all classes. Mrs. Stewart, going into her grocery store, heard the proprietor say to a gentleman, referring to her, "She is an Episcopalian, and will lose her situation." Upon inquiry she found that the denomination of Christians to which she belonged were unpopular with the Government, and were going to have nothing to do with the colored school. Without further inquiry Mrs. Stewart replied: "Well, before I will give up my religious sentiments for dollars and cents I will beg my bread from door to door." And she did almost beg her bread, as the sequel will show.

At the September term the teachers of several denominations assembled in their respective churches and received their appointments, while our heroine was left out in the cold. There were four other distinguished Episcopalians, one gentleman and three ladies, But they hid their light under a bushel and kept on the side of dollars and cents. The weather began to grow cool, and our heroine rented a room and paid two months' rent in advance; and then went to work and set herself about trying to get scholars, but met with poor success, not getting enough to pay expenses. The weather growing colder, the funds low, encountering cross looks, and sometimes unkind words, the distress of our heroine became extreme, so she called upon Judge Day, and he afforded her present relief for the time being.

Under all circumstances our heroine maintained a genteel appearance, and always attended the services of the church regularly every Sunday; but was a stranger in the city. Becoming acquainted with a colored lady belonging to the Church of the Asscension, our heroine related her condition to her. The lady recommended her to go and see her minister, the Rev. Dr. Hall,

"Oh! what can he do?" said the distressed one.

"Nothing beats a trial," was the reply.

So, in despair, after much persuasion, the two went together to see Dr. Hall; were kindly received; the tale of woe was told; Dr. Hall said he had no schools. The decision was the school was to be continued, if the supplicant could get scholars enough to supply her with food, which was almost doubtful. A Sunday school was to be established and a room rented at the expense of the church. The room was rented; a prayer meeting was formed; a Sunday school was established; a night school was opened, and a day school continued. Finally Christmas drew near; a five dollar bill was presented; a tree was purchased and dressed; benches were sent from the Epiphany. Forty persons were present at the celebration of the Saviour's birth. Dr. Hall was there; your heroine was there, and only one colored gentleman there to represent the colored Episcopalians in this city, This Christmas eve came on Saturday night. Notices were read in the different churches and put up on the east side of the house so they could be seen. Yet your heroine was a sufferer, with scarce the necessaries of life. The say was: "She belongs to white folks' church, let them take care of her." The curtain falls thus. and ends the scene.

But to return to my trip to Washington. I had prayed to the Lord that there might be standing by the cars some lad to conduct me where I wanted to go, for I was a perfect stranger. And upon my arrival, there stood a young man looking as if he wished he had something to do ; so when I alighted from the cars I went up to him and asked him if he was acquainted in the city. He answered yes. I told him if he would conduct me to where I wanted to go I would pay him for it ; so we went on and passed the White House. I was told on my way that Washington had become a perfect Paradise for the colored people since President Lincoln had taken his seat. I went to the city soon after the President had taken his seat. It was very dreary and dull, but I went on, trusting in the Lord, and found the minister's family I was looking for, and was welcomed, and made myself useful in the family until next spring. There was a lady, Mrs. Keckley, I knew, for- merly from Baltimore, who proved to be an ardent friend to me in my great emergency which took place afterward. I also had a letter of introduction to another lady, Miss M. F. Kiger, and got along very nicely, having no complaints to make, and was in the Nineteenth Street Baptist Church when the emancipation proclamation was read. Spring came ; the sun began to shine and the birds began to sing. I began to think about opening a school in the lower part of the city. And as I had promised to fight under Christ's banner against the world. the flesh, and the devil. and to be his faithful soldier and follower unto my life's end, I began to consider which church I should join. The min- ister of Trinity Church, Rev. Dr. Syle, was so much in sympathy with the South that an objection was raised by some of my Episcopalian friends from Baltimore. The colored people were not altogether pleased with the rector of Saint John's Church, Rev. Dr. Payne, before Dr. Lewis' time ; and although Dr. Hall was in sympathy with the South, he was considered the best man of the three ; in sympathy with the South because he had resided there ; it was thought natural that he should be. So I called upon Dr. Hall and placed myself under his parochial care. I saw by the papers Dr. Hall was very much spoken against. I said : "Doctor, the papers speak very hard of you." "Oh !" said he, "I do not read the papers." He lost his church ; it was used for Govern- ment purposes. Having just put myself under his Chris- tian care, I followed his flock to Willard's Hall, and there worshipped until he was again restored to his church. In the mean time I rented rooms, opened a school, and got along splendidly, until solicited by Judge Day and others to throw in my influence with theirs for the common good, and I should be paid by the month. I did so, and did it to my sorrow, as the sequel will show.

CHAPTER III.

But to return to the Christmas tree. The celebration of the Saviour's birth was celebrated in my school-room on Saturday night, which was rented of a man and his wife living in the same house; and the man said I could conduct my Christmas as I liked, and he was going to conduct his Christmas as he liked. On the Monday evening after, he said he was going to have music and dancing. I was horrified at the thought, and made arrangements to leave the house for the night, and locked up my room and went elsewhere. The next morning I met an Irish lady. Said she to me:

"Why don't you rent this nice little dwelling-house. It will cost you but little more than you pay now, and you ought not to live with such folks?"

"Why?" said I; "I did not know that you would rent the house to me."

"Yes I will," said she.

"I shall want prayer meeting, Sunday school, day school, and night school," said I.

"Oh," said she, "you can do just as you like, and have no one to trouble you."

So I moved forthwith. The house contained two fine-sized rooms, one up stairs and one down, and I always kept the house clean and in order. Every morning at nine o'clock it was ready for school, except Saturday; that day was devoted in arranging for the Sabbath. Every Sunday morning the house looked inviting for the scholars—the floor, the benches, the steps, and windows were always as clean as they could be. The scholars and teachers would come and work; would commence and end in time to get to church in season. I recollect the prayer meetings commenced under very adverse circumstances. Before I moved into the other house nothing was inviting. I was poor in the extreme; my stove was very small—not large enough to warm the room. I do not know how I did get along and where I got food to eat and fire to keep me and the children warm, what few

I had ; yet I was compelled to work after school hours, trying to get scholars to come either day or night, and people to come to prayer meeting at night ; and such was my extreme poverty that objection was raised to my having them at my room. No contributions were made to buy wood and coal. But Dr. Hall did his part ; he paid the rent, supplied the books. I had only five scholars in the day and as many or more at night. And that whole work was supported from these scholars I had night and day. Punctuality was always the life of business with me. One bitter cold night I prepared for prayer meeting, and made everything appear as cheerful as I could, but it began to grow so late I began to think nobody was coming. I had been after the only colored gentleman who took any interest in the matter, but he could not or would not come, although I told him Dr. Hall would be present ; so I returned to my lone room disappointed and sad. The bench was close to the stove, and I believe my floor was covered with an old carpet I had bought when I first went to Baltimore ; however, the fire looked dull, so I thought I would go and see the lady of the Ascension. But I had not gone far before I met Dr. Hall. The walking was very slippery, the ground was covered with snow and ice, it was a cold sleet. I thought Dr. Hall surely was a good man, or he would not be willing to come to so poor a person's house as were the people of whom I rented. I told him no one had come to the prayer meeting. He returned home, and called to tell the lady of the Ascension of my sorrow and disappointment.

CHAPTER IV.

But to my new house. I cannot tell when the appointment was made to change the prayer meetings to the different houses of the members. But I do know that when I had my prayer meeting the room would be nearly full, for I would go all around among the people and beg them to come ; and when the others had their prayer meetings they would not have any strangers, only their lone selves, and they did not appear to be so much better off than I was, either. There was another dear, Christian brother who fell in with us and invited us to his house to prayer meeting. He belonged to our faith and order, anyhow. And when we met, the lady of the house and the rest of the family retired and left the gentleman of the house, her husband, Dr. Hall, and a few others of us in a great big parlor, nicely fitted up, with a good fire, to carry on the prayer meeting by ourselves. I felt embarrassed for Dr. Hall at that time. He said he had a Colored Church South, with four hundred communicants, and he wanted to get up one here for the colored people. And no matter whom he was in sympathy with he was the principal man in laying the foundation of Saint Mary's Church. In the first place it was chiefly composed of females. But our representative brother was always with us, and by degrees others fell in. The prayer meeting and the Sunday school were under the Church of the Epiphany. Dr. Hall paid $10 toward the rent of the house, supplied the school with books and benches, I was to pay $2. Dr. Hall paid $10 for the one room. After I moved, the sisters contributed small sums toward getting wood and coal for Sunday school, but not much. My house was in the parish of the Trinity Church. Dr. Hall had to ask permission of the then rector of Trinity Church. I was the bearer of the note. So they both co-operated together. The prayer meeting was at my house once a week; and so one minister would come one evening one week and the other minister one evening the next week. Thus the prayer meetings at my house were conducted by the rector of the Epiphany and the rector of Trinity. All went on well for a while, and it thus went so far that a proposition was to be made to the vestry of Trinity to let the people have that small church on the corner of N and Sixth streets. And the rector of Trinity said I could teach school there; but an objection was made, for fear the boys would throw stones. And Dr. Hall said if the colored people would not have a church in that part of the city, he would have one at the west end, and he would dare any boys to throw stones at any work he had anything to do with. It was afterward sold to the Lutherans. It was an elegant little church; it belonged to Trinity. A lady said to me : "When we were getting up our church, we met in the same room for one year, and then we moved in a body ; but when you go from house to house, half of the persons do not know where the different places of meeting is."

Lent was about to commence. And the rector of Trinity was telling us how we must keep lent and use a reat deal of self denial about our food, &c. We had hirty-two present when the notice was given for the next meeting. I told the audience what the lady had said, ind asked them if they did not think it would be best to meet in one place until the body became consolidated. It was now in its embryo state. The lady of the Ascension and one of the ladies of the Epiphany, and I do not know how many more, were highly incensed, and went right straight to Dr. Hall and told him I wanted all the praise and credit of getting up the work; and cast my name out as evil all over the city as far as their circle extended; and broke up the prayer meetings. Dr. Hall said he would never come to my house again, and withdrew his rent money. He never came to my house again. No tongue can portray my agony of mind. I did not know what I should do, or how I should get along. I do not recollect whether my school increased in numbers or not. Still I kept on, turning neither to the right hand nor to the left. Ash Wednesday came. I went to church just as if nothing had happened. Oh! what a day that was. If I had had the wings of a dove I would indeed have flown to the utmost part of the earth. But I prayed God to show Dr. Hall in a vision, that I was a clean woman before the Lord; and I believe he did, as the end will show. Be that as it may, I made up my mind twice. Rather than to ask for any further aid I would starve to death. But God prevented it both times. The say would be: "Don't say you are an Episcopalian." And at last I went to see the Rev. Dr. Garnet of the Presbyterian Church. He blamed me for belonging to a set of unfeeling Christians. But he gave me one dollar and sent me to Dr. Channing, a Unitarian minister. I told Dr. Channing the circumstances in great distress of mind, walking the floor backward and forward. So he told me to come to him when the month was up and he would give me money to pay my rent or to go to my friends in New York. I went home. There were persons that were giving out to the poor. I did not go, for fear it would lessen the dignity of the Episcopal Church for it to be known that one of her members had to beg. It was a bitter cold night. I had to go and get some coal. I met a man and begged him to carry it for me to my house, for the cold almost overpowered me.

There were only two male members of the church that

I knew anything about. They were like Peter; they stood afar off to see the end. They seldom attended the church; and there were only a handfull of us poor lone colored women followers of the cross. More like the outcasts of the house of Israel than anything else. The proscription of the church at that time was awful. Sometimes she administered her communion to the blacks when they were at the table of the Lord, and sometimes she passed them by when they were at the table. My soul became filled with a holy indignation. I complained. And the result was the organization of Saint Mary's Church. Still I clung to the church. And had I left, no one would have cared. But by grace I overcame; and to-day am one of those that John saw in a vision on the Isle of Patmos having harps in their hands. I have suffered martyrdom for the church in one sense; and rejoice that I now feel that I have a home not only in the Protestant Episcopal Church, but in the Holy Church Catholic throughout the world.

CHAPTER V.

After I went to see the Rev. Dr. Garnet I think I began to get along better. But meeting the young lady (Miss M. F. Kiger) I brought the letter of introduction to, and looking poor in my apparel, I burst into tears and wept in the bitterness of my soul, and told her I did not think I should ever get along in Washington. She looked as if she pitied me from the bottom of her heart. I do not know what she said. But in three weeks' time I began to get along. All this suffering was in lent. Two Presbyterian ladies, Mrs. Slade and Keckley, came to my help; and they did not say "Be ye warmed and be ye fed" without affording the means; and one of them was the lady I was acquainted with in Baltimore. The other was a resident here. A lady from the John Wesley, Mrs. Tidball, was a staunch friend, and sent her child to school to me and paid in advance. The spring opened; my school increased. I went to see Dr. Channing at the time appointed. I told him I was beginning to get along so well I did not wish to leave Washington just then. He gave me $15. And a colored gentleman told me I must learn to manage, and said he wanted to rent my room up stairs. He paid me $6. I paid my rent; bought me a new shawl; went to the Church of the Epiphany every Sunday; kept my Sunday school, my day school, and my night school.

Dr. Hall sent the lady after me that had helped to make the fuss, but I think she had made an apology previously. And as I had committed my cause to Him who judgeth righteously, I said nothing about the past. She said Dr. Hall wished me to notify as many colored people as I could to come to the Church of the Epiphany on a certain evening named. He wanted to organize Saint Mary's Church. So I and thirteen night scholars went, and Dr. Hall said he would have the church organized right away. Two colored gentlemen present volunteered their services to help me teach the Sunday school, in order to forward the work. And when the church was consecrated we carried with us forty scholars and $2.50 the children had saved. Dr. Hall and Dr. Lewis were both waiting for us. And the services began after we entered the house.

Thus endeth my sorrows for the present.

RELIGION

INTRODUCTION.

This is the land of freedom. The press is at liberty.
Every man has a right to express his opinion. Many
think, because your skins are tinged with a sable hue,
that you are an inferior race of beings; but God does
not consider you as such. He hath formed and fashioned
you in His own glorious image, and hath bestowed upon
you reason and strong powers of intellect. He hath made
you to have dominion over the beasts of the field, the
fowls of the air, and the fishes of the sea. He hath
crowned you with glory and honor: hath made you but
a little lower than the angels; and, according to the
Constitution of these United States, he hath made all
men free and equal. Then why should one worm say to
another, "Keep you down there. while I sit up yonder;
for I am better than thou." It is not the color of the
skin that makes the man, but it is the principle formed
within the soul.

Many will suffer for pleading the cause of oppressed
Africa, and I shall glory in being one of her martyrs;
for I am firmly persuaded that the God in whom I trust
is able to protect me from the rage and malice of mine
enemies, and from them that will rise up against me;
and if there is no other way for me to escape, He is able
to take me to himself, as He did the most noble, fearless,
and undaunted David Walker.

NEVER WILL VIRTUE, KNOWLEDGE, AND TRUE POLITENESS
BEGIN TO FLOW TILL THE PURE PRINCIPLES OF RELIGION
AND MORALITY ARE PUT INTO FORCE.

My Respected Friends: I feel almost unable to address
you; almost incompetent to perform the task; and at
times I have felt ready to exclaim, O that my head were
waters and mine eyes a fountain of tears, that I might

veep day and night for the transgressions of the daughters of my people. Truly, my heart's desire and prayer is hat Ethiopia might stretch forth her hands unto God. But we have a great work to do. Never; no, never will he chains of slavery and ignorance burst till we become united as one and cultivate among ourselves the pure principles of piety, morality, and virtue. I am sensible of my ignorance; but such knowledge as God has given me I impart to you. I am sensible of former prejudices; but it is high time for prejudices and animosities to cease from among us. I am sensible of exposing myself to calumny and reproach; but shall I, for fear of feeble man who shall die, hold my peace? Shall I, for fear of scoffs and frowns, refrain my tongue? Ah, no! I speak as one that must give an account at the awful bar of God; I speak as a dying mortal, to dying mortals. O ye daughters of Africa, awake! awake! arise! no longer sleep nor slumber, but distinguish yourselves. Show forth to the world that ye are endowed with noble and exalted faculties. O ye daughters of Africa! what have ye done to immortalize your names beyond the grave? What examples have ye set before the rising generation? What foundation have ye laid for generations yet unborn? Where are our union and love? And where is our sympathy, that weeps at another's wo and hides the faults we see? And our daughters, where are they? Blushing in innocence and virtue! And our sons, do they bid fair to become crowns of glory to our hoary heads? Where is the parent who is conscious of having faithfully discharged his duty, and at the last awful day of account shall be able to say, here, Lord, is thy poor, unworthy servant and the children thou hast given me? And where are the children that will arise and call them blessed? Alas! O, God, forgive me if I speak amiss. The minds of our tender babes are tainted as soon as they are born; they go astray. as it were, from the womb. Where is the maiden who will blush at vulgarity? And where is the youth who has written upon his manly brow a thirst for knowledge; whose ambitious mind soars above trifles and longs for the time to come when he shall redress the wrongs of his father and plead the cause of his brethren? Did the daughters of our land possess a delicacy of manners, combined with gentleness and dignity? Did their pure minds hold vice in abhorrence

2

and contempt; did they frown when their ears were polluted with its vile accents, would not their influence become powerful? Would not our brethren fall in love with their virtues? Their souls would become fired with a holy zeal for freedom's cause. They would become ambitious to distinguish themselves; they would become proud to display their talents. Able advocates would arise in our defense. Knowledge would begin to flow, and the chains of slavery and ignorance would melt like wax before the flames. I am but a feeble instrument. I am but as one particle of the small dust of the earth. You may frown or smile. After I am dead, perhaps before, God will surely raise up those who will more powerfully and eloquently plead the cause of virtue and the pure principles of morality than I am able to do. O, virtue, how sacred is thy name; how pure are thy principles. Who can find a virtuous woman? for her price is far above rubies. Blessed is the man who shall call her his wife; yea, happy is the child who shall call her mother. O, woman, woman, would thou only strive to excel in merit and virtue; would thou only store thy mind with useful knowledge. great would be thine influence. Do you say you are too far advanced in life now to begin? You are not too far advanced to instil these principles into the minds of your tender infants. Let them by no means be neglected. Discharge your duty faithfully in every point of view; leave the event with God. So shall your skirts become clear of their blood.

When I consider how little improvement has been made the last eight years; the apparent cold and indifferent state of the children of God; how few have been hopefully brought to the knowledge of the truth as it is in Jesus; that our young men and maidens are fainting and drooping, as it were, by the way side for the want of knowledge; when I see how few care to distinguish themselves either in religious or moral improvement, and when I see the greater part of our community following the vain bubbles of life with so much eagerness, which will only prove to them like the serpent's sting upon the bed of death, I really think we are in as wretched and miserable a state as was the house of Israel in the days of Jeremiah.

I suppose many of my friends will say "religion is all your theme." I hope my conduct will ever prove to me to be what I profess, a true follower of Christ. And it is the religion of Jesus alone that will constitute your happiness here and support you in a dying hour. O, then, do not trifle with God and your own souls any longer. Do not presume to offer him the very dregs of your lives; but now, whilst you are blooming in health and vigor, consecrate the remnant of your days to him. Do you wish to become useful in your day and generation? Do you wish to promote the welfare and happiness of your friends as far as your circle extends? Have you one desire to become truly great? O, then, become truly pious, and God will endow you with wisdom and knowledge from on high.

> Come, turn to God, who did thee make,
> And at his presence fear and quake;
> Remember him now in thy youth.
> And let thy soul take hold of truth.
>
> The devil and his ways defy,
> Believe him not, he doth but lie;
> His ways seem sweet: but, youth, beware!
> He for thy soul hath laid a snare.

Religion is pure; it is ever new; it is beautiful; it is all that is worth living for. O, could I but see the church built up in the most holy faith; could I but see men spiritually minded, walking in the fear of God, not given to filthy lucre, not holding religion in one hand and the world in the other, but diligent in business, fervent in spirit, serving the Lord, standing upon the walls of Zion, crying to passers by: "Ho, every one that thirsteth, come ye to the waters, and he that hath no money; yea, come and buy wine and milk without money and without price; turn ye, turn ye, for why will ye die?" Could I but see mothers in Israel, chaste, keepers at home, not busy bodies, meddlers in other men's matters, whose adorning is of the inward man, possessing a meek and quiet spirit, whose sons were like olive-plants, and whose daughters were as polished corner-stones; could I but see young men and maidens turning their feet from impious ways, rather choosing to suffer affliction with the people of God than to enjoy the pleasures of sin for a season; could I but see the rising youth blushing in artless innocence, then could I say, now, Lord, let thine unworthy handmaiden depart in peace, for I have seen the desire of mine eyes, and am satisfied.

O, Lord God, the watchmen of Zion have cried peace, peace, when there was no peace; they have been, as it were, blind leaders of the blind. Wherefore hast thou so long withheld from us the divine influences of thy Holy Spirit? Wherefore hast thou hardened our hearts and blinded our eyes? It is because we have honored thee with our lips, when our hearts were far from thee. We have polluted thy Sabbaths, and even our most holy things have been solemn mockery to thee. We have regarded iniquity in our hearts, therefore thou wilt not hear. Return again unto us, O, Lord God, we beseech thee, and pardon this, the iniquity of thy servants. Cause thy face to shine upon us, and we shall be saved. O visit us with thy salvation. Raise up sons and daughters unto Abraham, and grant that there might come a mighty shaking of dry bones among us, and a great ingathering of souls. Quicken thy professing children. Grant that the young man may be constrained to believe that there is a reality in religion, and a beauty in the fear of the Lord. Have mercy on the benighted sons and daughters of Africa. Grant that we may soon become so distinguished for our moral and religious improvements, that the nations of the earth may take knowledge of us; and grant that our cries may come up before thy throne like holy incense. Grant that every daughter of Africa may consecrate her sons to thee from the birth. And do thou, Lord, bestow upon them wise and understanding hearts. Clothe us with humility of soul, and give us a becoming dignity of manners; may we imitate the character of the meek and lowly Jesus; and do thou grant that Ethiopia may soon stretch forth her hands unto thee. And now, Lord, be pleased to grant that Satan's kingdom may be destroyed; that the kingdom of our Lord Jesus Christ may be built up; that all nations, and kindreds, and tongues, and people might be brought to the knowledge of the truth, as it is in Jesus, and we at last meet around thy throne, and join in celebrating thy praises. ·

———

I have been taking a survey of the American people in my own mind, and I see them thriving in arts, and sciences, and in polite literature. Their highest aim is to excel in political, moral, and religious improvement. They early consecrate their children to God, and their youth

, indeed are blushing in artless innocence ; they wipe the
tears from the orphan's eyes, and they cause the widow's
heart to sing for joy ; and their poorest ones, who have
the least wish to excel, they promote. And those that
have but one talent, they encourage. But how very few
are there among them that bestow one thought upon the
benighted sons and daughters of Africa, who have enriched the soils of America with their tears and blood ;
few to promote their cause, none to encourage their talents.
Under these circumstances, do not let our hearts be any
longer discouraged ; it is no use to murmur nor to repine.
but let us promote ourselves and improve our own talents.
And I am rejoiced to reflect that there are many able and
talented ones among us whose names might be recorded
on the bright annals of fame. But, " *I can't*," is a great
barrier in the way. I hope it will soon be removed, and
" *I will.*" resume its place. ◀

Righteousness exalteth a nation, but sin is a reproach
to any people. Why is it, my friends, that our minds
have been blinded by ignorance to the present moment?
Tis on account of sin. Why is it that our church is involved in so much difficulty? It is on account of sin.
Why is it that God has cut down, upon our right hand
and upon our left the most learned and intelligent of
our men? O, shall I say, it is on account of sin ! Why
is it that thick darkness is mantled upon every brow, and
we, as it were, look sadly upon one another? It is on
account of sin. O, then, let us bow before the Lord our
God, with all our hearts, and humble our very souls in
the dust before him ; sprinkle, as it were, ashes upon our
heads, and awake to righteousness, and sin not. The arm
of the Lord is not shortened, that it cannot save ; neither
is his ear heavy, that he cannot hear ; but it is your iniquities that have separated you from me, saith the Lord.
Return, O ye backsliding children, and I will return unto
you. and ye shall be my people, and I will be your God.

O, ye mothers, . what a responsibility rests on you !
You have souls committed to your charge, and God will
require a strict account of you. It is you that must
create in the minds of your little girls and boys a thirst
for knowledge, the love of virtue, the abhorrence of vice.
and the cultivation of a pure heart. The seeds thus sown
will grow with their growing years ; and the love of virtue

thus early formed in the soul will protect their inexpe-rienced feet from many dangers. O, do not say, you cannot make anything of your children; but say, with the help and assistance of God, we will try. Do not indulge them in their little stubborn ways; for a child left to himself bringeth his mother to shame. Spare not, for their crying; thou shalt beat them with a rod and they shall not die; and thou shall save their souls from hell. When you correct them, do it in the fear of God, and for their own good. They will not thank you for your false and foolish indulgence; they will rise up, as it were, and curse you in this world; and, in the world to come, condemn you. It is no use to say, you can't do this, or, you can't do that: you will not tell your Maker so, when you meet him at the great day of account. And you must be careful that you set an example worthy of following, for you they will imitate. There are many instances, even among us now, where parents have discharged their duty faithfully, and their children now reflect honor upon their gray hairs.

Perhaps you will say, that many parents have set pure examples at home, and they have not followed them. True, our expectations are often blasted; but let us not dishearten you. If they have faithfully discharged their duty, even after they are dead, their works may live; their prodigal children may then return to God, and become heirs of salvation; if not, their children cannot rise and condemn them at the awful bar of God.

Perhaps you will say, that you cannot send them to high schools and academies. You can have them taught in the first rudiments of useful knowledge, and then you can have private teachers, who will instruct them in the higher branches; and their intelligence will become greater than ours, and their children will attain to higher advantages, and *their* children still higher; and then, though we are dead, our works shall live; though we are mouldering, our names shall not be forgotten.

Finally, my heart's desire and prayer to God is, that there might come a thorough reformation among us. Our minds have too long grovelled in ignorance and sin. Come, let us incline our ears to wisdom, and apply our hearts to understanding; promote her, and she shall exalt thee; she shall bring thee to honor when thou dost embrace her. An ornament of grace shall she be to thy

head, and a crown of glory shall she deliver to thee.
Take fast hold of instruction; let her not go; keep her,
for she is thy life. Come, let us turn unto the Lord our
God, with all our heart and soul, and put away every un-
clean and unholy thing from among us, and walk before
the Lord our God, with a perfect heart, all the days of
our lives; then we shall be a people with whom God shall
delight to dwell; yea, we shall be that happy people
whose God is the Lord.

I am of a strong opinion, that the day on which we
unite, heart and soul, and turn our attention to knowledge and improvement, that day the hissing and reproach
among the nations of the earth against us will cease.
And even those who now point at us with the finger of
scorn, will aid and befriend us. It is of no use for us to
sit with our hands folded, hanging our heads like bul-
rushes, lamenting our wretched condition; but let us
make a mighty effort, and arise; and if no one will promote or respect us, let us promote and respect ourselves.

The American ladies have the honor conferred on them,
that by prudence and economy in their domestic concerns, and their unwearied attention in forming the
minds and manners of their children, they laid the foundation of their becoming what they now are. The good
women of Wethersfied, Conn., toiled in the blazing sun.
year after year, weeding onions, then sold the seed and
procured money enough to erect them a house of worship;
and shall we not imitate their examples, as far as they are
worthy of imitation? Why cannot we do something to
distinguish ourselves, and contribute some of our hard
earnings that would reflect honor upon our memories,
and cause our children to arise and call us blessed?
Shall it any longer be said of the daughters of Africa,
they have no ambition, they have no force? By no
means. Let every female heart become united; and let
us raise a fund ourselves; and at the end of one year
and a half, we might be able to lay the corner-stone for
the building of a High School, that the higher branches
of knowledge might be enjoyed by us; and God would
raise us up, and enough to aid us in our laudable designs.
Let each one strive to excel in good housewifery, knowing that prudence and economy are the road to wealth.
Let us not say, we know this, or, we know that, and practice nothing; but let us practice what we do know.

How long shall the fair daughters of Africa be compelled to bury their minds and talents beneath a load of iron pots and kettles? Until union, knowledge, and love begin to flow among us. How long shall a mean set of men flatter us with their smiles, and enrich themselves with our hard earnings; their wives' fingers sparkling with rings, and they themselves laughing at our folly? Until we begin to promote and patronize each other. Shall we be a mere by-word among the nations any longer? Shall they laugh us to scorn forever? Do you ask, what can we do? Unite and build a store of your own, if you cannot procure a license. Fill one side with dry-goods and the other with groceries. Do you ask, where is the money? We have spent more than enough for nonsense to do what building we should want. We have never had an opportunity of displaying our talents; therefore the world thinks we know nothing. And we have been possessed of by far too mean and cowardly a disposition, though I highly disapprove of an insolent or impertinent one. Do you ask the disposition I would have you possess? Possess the spirit of independence. The Americans do, and why should not you? Possess the spirit of men, bold and enterprising, fearless and undaunted. Sue for your rights and privileges. Know the reason that you cannot attain them. Weary them with your importunities. You can but die, if you make the attempt; and we shall certainly die if you do not. The Americans have practiced nothing but head-work these 200 years, and we have done their drudgery. And is it not high time for us to imitate their examples, and practice head-work too, and keep what we have got, and get what we can? We need never to think that anybody is going to feel interested for us, if we do not feel interested for ourselves. That day we, as a people, hearken unto the voice of the Lord our God, and walk in his ways and ordinances, and become distinguished for our ease, elegance, and grace, combined with other virtues—that day the Lord will raise us up, and enough to aid and befriend us, and we shall begin to flourish.

Were every gentleman in America to realize as one that they had got to become bondmen, and their wives, their sons, and their daughters servants forever to Great Britain, like Belshazzar, their joints would become loosened, and tremblingly would smite one against another; their countenance would be filled with horror, every nerve and muscle would be forced into action; their souls would recoil at the very thought, their hearts would die within them, and death would be far more preferable. Then why have not Afric's sons a right to feel the same? Are not their wives, their sons, and their daughters as dear to them as those of the white man's? Certainly God has not deprived them of the divine influences of his Holy Spirit, which is the greatest of all blessings, if they ask him. Then why should man any longer deprive his fellow man of equal rights and privileges? O, America, America, foul and indelible is thy stain! Dark and dismal is the cloud that hangs over thee for thy cruel wrongs and injuries to the fallen sons of Africa. The blood of her murdered ones cries to heaven for vengeance against thee. Thou art almost become drunken with the blood of her slain; thou hast enriched thyself through her toils and labors; and now thou refuseth to make even a small return. And thou hast caused the daughters of Africa to commit whordoms and fornications; but upon thee be their curse.

O, ye great and mighty men of America, ye rich and powerful ones, many of you will call for the rocks and mountains to fall upon you, and to hide you from the wrath of the lamb, and from him that sitteth upon the throne; whilst many of the sable-skinned Africans you now despise, will shine in the kingdom of heaven as the stars, forever and ever. Charity begins at home, and those that provide not for their own, are worse than infidels. We know that you are raising contributions to aid the gallant Poles; we know that you have befriended Greece and Ireland; and you have rejoiced with France for her heroic deeds of valor. You have acknowledged all the nations of the earth, except Hayti; and you may publish, as far as the East is from the West, that you have two millions of negroes, who aspire no higher than to bow at your feet and to court your smiles. You may kill, tyrannize and oppress as much as you choose, until our cry shall come up before the throne of God; for I am firmly persuaded that he will not suffer you to quell the proud, fearless and undaunted spirit of the Africans forever; for in his own time, he is able to plead his own cause against you, and to pour out upon you the ten

2*

plagues of Egypt. We will not come out against you with swords and staves, as against a thief; but we will tell you that our souls are fired with the same love of liberty and independence with which your souls are fired. We will tell you that too much of your blood flows in our veins, and too much of your color in our skins, for us not to possess your spirits. We will tell you that it is our gold that clothes you in fine linen and purple, and causes you to fare sumptuously every day; and it is the blood of our fathers and the tears of our brethren that have enriched your soils. *And we claim our rights.* We will tell you that we are not afraid of them that kill the body, and after that can do no more; but we will tell you whom we do fear. We fear Him who is able, after he hath killed, to destroy both soul and body in hell forever. Then, my brethren, sheath your swords, and calm your angry passions. Stand still, and know that the Lord he is God. Vengeance is his, and he will repay. It is a long lane that has no turn. America has-risen to her meridian. When you begin to thrive, she will begin to fall. God hath raised you up a Walker and a Garrison. Though Walker sleeps, yet he lives, and his name shall be held in everlasting remembrance. I, even I, who am but a child, inexperienced to any of you, am a living witness to testify unto you this day, that I have seen the wicked in great power, spreading himself like a green bay tree, and lo, he passed away; yea, I diligently sought him, but he could not be found; and it is God alone that has inspired my heart to feel for Afric's woes. Then fret not yourself because of evil doers. Fret not yourself because of the men who bring wicked devices to pass, for they shall be cut down as the grass, and wither as the green herb. Trust in the Lord, and do good; so shalt thou dwell in the land, and verily thou shalt be fed. Encourage the noble-hearted Garrison. Prove to the world that you are neither ourang-outangs, nor a species of mere animals, but that you possess the same powers of intellect as those of the proud-boasting American.

I am sensible, my brethren and-friends, that many of you have been deprived of advantages, kept in utter ignorance, and that your minds are now darkened; and if any of you have attempted to aspire after high and noble enterprises, you have met with so much opposition that your souls have become discouraged. For this very cause a few of us have ventured to expose our lives in your behalf, to plead your cause against the great; and it will be of no use, unless you feel for yourselves and your little ones, and exhibit the spirits of men. O, then, turn your attention to knowledge and improvement; for knowledge is power. And God is able to fill you with wisdom and understanding, and to dispel your fears. Arm yourselves with the weapons of prayer. Put your trust in the living God. Persevere strictly in the paths of virtue. Let nothing be lacking on your part, and in God's own time, and his time is certainly the best, he will surely deliver you with a mighty hand and with an outstretched arm.

I have never taken one step, my friends, with a design to raise myself in your esteem or to gain applause. But what I have done has been done with an eye single to the glory of God, and to promote the good of souls. I have neither kindred nor friends. I stand alone in your midst, exposed to the fiery darts of the devil, and to the assaults of wicked men. But though all the powers of earth and hell were to combine against me, though all nature should sink into decay, still would I trust in the Lord, and joy in the God of salvation. For I am fully persuaded that he will bring me off conqueror; yea, more than conqueror, through him who hath loved me and given himself for me.

Boston, *October*, 1831.

MEDITATIONS.

INTRODUCTION.

Tell me no more of earthly toys,
Of sensual mirth and carnal joys,
For these are trifling things

Once more I am about to make a feeble effort, in presenting the meditations of my heart before my friends and the public. I am sensible that my writings show forth the want of knowledge, and that they are scarce worthy of a perusal. But as I have said before, I say again, such knowledge as God giveth to me, I impart to you.

The author has, as it were, upon the one hand, basked in the sunshine of prosperity; and on the other, she has drunk deep in the cup of sorrow.

Never did I realize, till I was forced to, that it was from God I derived every earthly blessing, and that it was God who had a right to take them away. I found it almost impossible to say, "Thy will be done." It is now one year since Christ first spoke peace to my troubled soul. Soon after I presented myself before the Lord in the holy ordinance of baptism, my soul became filled with holy meditations and sublime ideas; and my ardent wish and desire have ever been, that I might become a humble instrument in the hands of God, of winning some poor souls to Christ. Though I am sensible that Paul may plant, and Apollos water, but that God alone giveth the increase, through Christ strengthening me I can do all things; without him I can do nothing.

It appears to me that because sin abounds, the love of many have waxed cold; and I cannot believe that God would have so long withheld the divine influences of his Holy spirit from this people, had the professing followers of Christ more faithfully defended the cause of their blessed Lord and Master; for he has said that he will be inquired of by the house of Israel to do those things for them that they need. I have borrowed much of my language from the Holy Bible. During the years of childhood and youth it was the black book that I mostly studied; and now, while my hands are toiling for their daily sustenance, my heart is most generally meditating upon its divine truths. I am more and more convinced that the cause of Christ will never be built up, Satan's kingdom will never be destroyed, the chains of slavery and ignorance will never burst, and morality and virtue will never flourish, till pure and holy examples are set home, and the professing followers of Christ arise and shine forth, and prove to the world that there is a reality in religion, and a beauty in the fear of the Lord.

MEDITATION I.

My Friends: I have been sorely troubled in my mind; and why? It is because I have seen that many who have professed the name of Christ are not careful to discharge their duty faithfully to their dying fellow immortals around them. I have been considering that it will be but a poor excuse for me to say, when I appear at the awful bar of God, that the reason I neglected my duty was because I was faithful that this one would frown upon me and that one would smile. Religion has become too fashionable and too unpopular even among the professing followers of Christ. O, how will they feel in that day to see their skirts filled with the blood of souls? Will not their eye-balls start from their sockets to see sinners who have stumbled into hell over them? and will not their hearts be rent in twain to hear them in anguish condemn them? "If thou warn not the wicked man to flee from his ways and he die in his sins, his blood will I require at thy hand, saith the Lord of hosts." O, the value of time! O, the worth of immortal souls! The harvest indeed is plenteous, but the laborers are few. Pray ye, therefore, to the Lord of the harvest that he would send forth faithful laborers into his vineyard.

My respected friends. I have indeed found that the Christian life is a life of warfare; for the spirit wars against the flesh, and the flesh against the spirit; and I am forced to cry out with St. Paul, from time to time, "O, wretched man that I am! who shall deliver me from this body of sin and death! for the good that I would do, that I do not; and the evil that I would not do, that I do!"

MEDITATION II.

How pleased and blest was I,
To hear the people cry:
Come, let us seek for God to-day;
Yes, with a cheerful zeal,
We'll haste to Zion's hill,
And there our vows and honors pay.

How amiable are thy tabernacles, O Lord of hosts, and the place where thine honor dwelleth! Truly, I can say with the Psalmist that I had rather be a door-keeper in the house of my God than to dwell in the tents of wickedness. What a sublimity dwells among the assemblies of thy saints! Truly thine abodes of worship are none other than the very gates of heaven. The sun has risen gloriously upon the earth. O that its rays might shine into this benighted soul of mine. Soon I shall be laid in the silent tomb or beneath the sod; and the places that know me now will know me no more forever. Then, O my soul, improve thy Sabbaths, and waste not their precious hours. Grant that what I hear this day, O God, may not be as water spilt upon the ground, which cannot be gathered up; but may be as good seed sown in the heart, springing up unto life eternal.

I have just returned from church. The discourse made

a deep and solemn impression on my mind. O, may what I have heard prove a rich and lasting blessing to my soul. Disrobe me, O God, of every impure and unholy affection, and make my soul a fit temple for thee to dwell in.

PRAYER.

O thou King eternal, immortal, invisible, and only wise God, before whom angels bow and seraphs veil their faces, crying, holy, holy, holy is the Lord God Almighty. True and righteous are thy ways, thou King of saints. Help me, thy poor unworthy creature, humbly to prostrate myself before thee, and implore that mercy which my sins have justly forfeited. O God, I know that I am not worthy of a place at thy footstool; but to whom shall I go but unto thee? Thou alone hast the words of eternal life. Send me not away without a blessing, I beseech thee; but enable me to wrestle like Jacob, and to prevail like Israel. Be graciously pleased, O God, to pardon all that thou hast seen amiss in me this day, and enable me to live more to thine honor and glory for the time to come. Bless the church to which I belong, and grant that when thou makest up thy jewels not one soul shall be found missing. Bless him in whom thou hast set over us as a watchman in Zion. Let not his soul be discouraged. May he not fail to declare the whole counsel of God, whether sinners will hear or forbear. And now, Lord, what wait I for? My hope is in thee. Do more for me than I can possibly ask or think, and finally receive me to thyself.

MEDITATION III.

My friends, I have been brought to consider that it is because the Lord he is God that I have not been consumed. It is because that his tender compassion fails not, that I am not now in hell lifting up my eyes in torments, where the worm dieth not and where the fire is not quenched. And I cannot help but exclaim, glory to God that I am a prisoner of hope. I rejoice that I have been formed a rational and accountable creature, and that ever I was born to be born again. I rejoice that the Lord God omnipotent reigneth, and that he searches the hearts and tries the reins of the children of men. When I sin I feel that I have an advocate with the Father, even Jesus Christ, the righteous, who was in all points tempted like unto ourselves, yet without sin. He knows what sore temptations mean, for he has felt the same; and with his supporting grace I am determined to resist the lusts of the world, the flesh, and the devil, and to fight the good fight of faith and win the crown, and by my Father's side sit down. Choose ye this day, therefore, whom ye will serve; but as for me, I am determined to serve the Lord.

MEDITATION IV.

Afflicted saints to Christ draw near,
The Saviour's gracious promise hear;
His gracious words declare to thee,
That as thy days, thy strength shall be.

Why art thou cast down, O my soul, why art thou disquieted within me? Hope thou in God, for I shall yet praise him. Have just returned from church meeting. Did not perceive that Christian spirit of fellowship which ought to exist. Is there an Achan among us, O God, who has done the accursed thing; or is there a Jonah among us who has refused to obey thy will? If not, why hast thou so long hid thy face from us? for we are consumed by thine anger, and by thy wrath are we troubled. Return again unto us, O Lord God, we beseech thee, and open the eyes of our understanding, that we may see wherein we have sinned against thee. O God, we have robbed thee, in not presenting thee the first offering of our hearts. O turn away from us thy fierce anger, and pardon this our iniquity, and lift upon us more the light of thou reconciled countenance, and the joy of thy salvation. Have met with an earthly disappointment. Am somewhat disheartened. Naked came I forth from my mother's womb, naked shall I return thither. The Lord gave and the Lord hath taken away: blessed be the name of the Lord. O my soul, labor not for the meat that perisheth, but for that which endureth unto life eternal. Lord, thou hast chastened me sore; but though thou hast caused me to fall, thou hast not utterly taken from me thy loving kindness: but thou hast dealt in tender mercy and compassion with me. I adore thee, praise thee, and bless thee, Parent of mercies, for thy patience and forbearance with me; for hadst thou left me to myself, where would my mad career have ended? Parent of mercies, give me calm submission to thy holy will in all things; for thou hast said that as thy day is so shall thy strength be.

PRAYER.

Our Father, which art in heaven, hallowed be thy name.
Thy kingdom come. Thy will be done. Enable me to
say from my heart, Thy will be done, O God. The heaven
is thy throne and the earth is thy footstool; neither may
any say unto thee, what doest thou? But thou art the
high and lofty One that inhabiteth eternity, yet will thou
condescend to look upon him that is of a humble, a broken,
and a contrite heart. As such, enable me, O God, to bow
before thee at this time, under a deep sense of my guilt
and unworthiness. It was my sins that caused thee to
arise in thy wrath against me. Be pleased, O God, to
blot them from thy book, and remember them no more
forever. Bless the church to which I belong. Thine
arm is not shortened that it cannot save, neither is thine
ear heavy that it cannot hear; but it is our sins that have
separated thee from us. Purge us from all our dross;
hide thy face from our iniquities, and speak peace to our
troubled souls. Bless thy servant, our pastor; let not his
soul be discouraged, but may an angel appear unto him
strengthening him. Bless all the benighted sons and
daughters of Africa, especially my unconverted friends.
Send them not away from thy presence into that lake
that burneth with fire and brimstone; but magnify the
riches of thy grace in plucking their souls as brands from
the burning; and though I may long sleep in death before thou wilt perform this work, yet grant that in the
resurrection morn we may all awake in thy likeness and
our souls be bound in the sure bundle of eternal life.

MEDITATION V.

I have been contemplating that if we live pure and virtuous lives here, when we come upon the bed of death
we shall be enabled to lean our head upon the bosom of
Jesus, and to breathe our souls out sweetly there. He
will safely carry us through the dark valley of the shadow
of death, and angels will convey us to heaven. There we
shall sit down with Abraham and Isaac and Jacob, and
with the spirits of just men made perfect. There the
Lord God will wipe away tears from all our faces, and
we shall join with the hundred and forty-four thousand
in singing the song of Moses and the Lamb:

> Worthy the Lamb that died, they cry,
> To be exalted thus!
> Worthy the Lamb, our lips reply,
> For he was slain for us!

.My Christian friends, let us examine ourselves, and pray for peace of conscience, joy in the Holy Ghost, increase of grace, and perseverence there unto the end.

MEDITATION VI.

Before we proceed any father, permit me to ask you, my Christian friends, in the name of the Lord Jesus Christ, what progress are you making in the divine life? Are you bringing forth the fruits of righteousness, and proving to the world by your own conduct that there is a reality in religion, and a beauty in the fear of the Lord? Are you letting your light so shine before men that they may see your good works and glorify your Father which is in heaven? Christ has said that he is more willing to give his Holy Spirit to them that ask him, than earthly parents are to bestow good gifts upon their children ; and that if two or three shall ask anything in his name, believing that he is able to perform, it shall be done for them of their Father which is in heaven ; and certainly the fervent, effectual prayer of the righteous availeth much. O, then, shall precious and immortal souls perish through our neglect? Shall they stumble into hell over us, and rise up in judgment and condemn us? Is it not to be feared that many who profess the name of Jesus at the present day are much like the whited sepulchres, which indeed appear beautiful without, but inwardly are full of all manner of uncleanliness? Do not many love the praise of man more than the praise of God? Have we not all been unprofitable servants? And is it not to be feared that at the great and terrible day of the Lord he will arise and shut the door? and many will stand without and begin to knock and say, Lord. Lord, open unto us ; but he will say, I know not from whence ye are : depart from me. ye workers of iniquity. And soon the summons will go forth against you, my unconverted friends ; cut them down, for why cumber they the ground? Christ has been seeking fruit of you these many years, and lo, he hath found none. O, how can you go on, year after year, and month after month, sinning against a holy and a righteous God, who is constantly showering down the choicest of his blessings upon you? O, how can you see your friends dropping into the eternal world. and yet feel no concern for your never-dying souls? Will not the terrors of death alarm you, the horrors of hell affright you, nor the calls and invitations of mercy persuade you? Come now, saith the Lord, and let us reason together; though your own sins have been as scarlet, they shall be made as wool; and though they have been red like crimson, they shall become whiter than snow. O, my friends, believe me or not, I have felt at times to exclaim with Moses: O, Lord God, this people have sinned a great sin; but now if thou wilt forgive them, blot me, I pray thee, from thy book. And the Lord said: Him that sinneth against me, him will I blot from my book.

MEDITATION VII.

At his presence nature shakes,
  Earth affrighted hastes to flee;
Solid mountains melt like wax,
  What will then become of thee?

O, my unconverted friends, where will you hide yourselves in the great and terrible day of the Lord? Where will you secrete yourselves from the presence of the Almighty? If you ascend into heaven, he is there; if you make your bed in hell, he is there. If you take the wings of the morning and fly to the utmost parts of the earth, even there shall he find you, and his right hand shall search you out. Be not deceived, God is not mocked. If the righteous are scarcely saved, where will the sinner and the ungodly appear? Now consider this, ye that forget God, lest he tare you in pieces, and there is none to deliver you.

Where now their haughty looks?
  O. their horror and despair.
When they see the open books,
  And the dreadful sentence hear!

O, friends, it is painful to tell you the truth, but you had better hear it now before it is eternally too late. O, then, fly to the Saviour before the door of mercy is forever shut against you. Repent and believe in the Lord Jesus Christ, and thou shalt be saved.

PRAYER.

O, Lord God, Paul may plant, and Apollos water, but thou alone givest the increase. We are sensible that without thee we can do nothing. Vain are all our efforts without thy blessing. But, O Lord God, thou hast the hearts of all thy creatures in hand, and thou canst turn them withersoever thou wilt. Strip the hearts of this people from their idols, we humbly beseech thee. Take off their eyes from beholding vanity. Thou canst glorify thyself in making them the monuments of thy mercy; and thou canst glorify thyself in making them the monuments of thy wrath. Glorify thyself in making them the monuments of thy victorious grace. Open their eyes that they may see that their feet stand upon slippery places, and that fiery billows roll beneath them. And, O Lord God, wilt thou in an especial manner have mercy on our unconverted brethren? Soften their proud and rebellious hearts, and be not angry with them forever. O, Jesus of Nazareth, hast thou not died that they might live? Hast thou not become poor that they might become rich? Is not thy blood sufficient to atone? Wherefore, O Lord God, hast thou hardened their hearts and blinded their eyes? Wherefore hast thou so long withheld from them the divine influences of thy holy spirit? Open their eyes that they may see that they are going down to hell as fast as the wheels of time can carry them. O, stop them in their mad career! Grant that a grievous cry might be heard among thy professing children in behalf of perishing souls; and may it be like the cry of the Egyptians in the night that thou didst slay their firstborn. And not only for ourselves do we pray, but for all nations, kindreds, tongues, and people. Grant that an innumerable host, which no man can number, may be gathered in from the four winds of heaven; and when the last trumpet shall sound. grant that we may be caught up into the clouds of the air and our ear saluted with the joyful sound: "Well done, thou good and faithful servant; thou hast been faithful over a few things, I will make the ruler over many things; enter thou into the joy of thy Lord."

MEDITATION VIII.

Is there no balm in Gilead, and is there no physician there? Yes, there is balm in Gilead and there is a physician there. And O, my soul, thou hast found that physician, and he hath applied his healing medicines to thy bleeding heart, and hath cured the of thy wounds. Come, then, all ye mourning souls to this physician; he alone can heal your maladies. Are you poor? He is inexhaustibly rich and benevolent, and will heal you without money and without price. Is your case a desperate one? Are you full of wounds, and bruises, and putrefying sores? Come just as you are. Look steadfastly to him, believe in his skill, and you shall be made whole,

Another year is past and gone forever. Have been deeply impsessed on account of past sins and ingratitude. But methinks I hear a voice, which says: Blessed are they that mourn, for they shall be comforted. Methinks I hear a voice, which says: Daughter, be of good cheer; thy sins be forgiven thee. Consoling thought! O, thou compassionate Redeemer, was it love that induced thee to leave the realms of bliss, and take upon thee the form of a servant, and descend into this lower world, to die for fallen man? Infinite love! Amazing condescension! A mystery, indeed, that the angels desire to look into. Even eternity will be too short for blood-washed millions to celebrate thy praises.

PRAYER.

O, thou sin-forgiving God, they that are whole need not a physician, but they that are sick. Lord, I am sick, and full of diseases. If thou wilt, thou canst make me clean. Though my sins have been as scarlet, thou canst make them as wool; and though they be read like crimson, thou canst make them whiter than snow. Were it not that there is a sufficiency in thy blood to atone for the vilest, the view of my past sins and transgressions would sink me in despair. But thou hast said, him that cometh to thee thou wilt in no wise cast out. Lord, I come, pleading alone the merits of my Redeemer; not only for myself do I plead, but for the whole race of mankind—especially for the benighted sons and daughters of Africa. Do thou loose their bonds, and let the oppressed go free. Bless thy churches throughout the whole world. Clothe thy ministers with salvation, and cause thy saints to shout for joy. Grant that the time may soon come that all may know thee, from the rising of the sun unto the going down thereof. In an especial manner wilt thou look down upon the church to which I belong. Fire our souls with a holy zeal for thy cause. and let us not rest at ease in Zion whilst souls are perishing for the lack of knowledge. Wilt thou increase her number of such, and such only, as shall be saved. Bless our pastor with a double portion of thy Spirit. Encourage his heart, and strehgthen him in the inward man. and may he see the work of the Lord prosper in his hands. And now, Lord, what wait I for? Dispel every gloomy fear that pervades my mind, and enable me to hope in thy mercy, and to thee will I ascribe praises everlasting.

MEDITATION IX.

I have been impressed in my mind, my unconverted friends, with the awful idea that God is about to execute upon us the fierceness of his anger, and to pour forth heavy judgments upon this people. And why? Because your sins have reached unto heaven, and your iniquities unto the clouds. God has been calling you these many years to repentance, by his loving kindness and tender mercies; and Christ has been knocking at the door of your hearts for admittance, until his locks have become wet with the dews of heaven. Nay, even more; he hath chastened you with the rod of his wrath, and hath deprived you of your kindred and friends; he hath sent death and pestilence among you, and many have become widows, and their children fatherless; and still you go on unconcerned, as though all were well, saying, with proud Pharaoh: "Who is the Lord, that we should obey him?" You have closed your eyes against the light; you have stopped your ears against the truth; and you have hardened your hearts against the calls and invitations of mercy; and I am fearful that the Queen of the South will arise in judgment against this generation and condemn it—for she came from the uttermost parts of the earth to hear of the wisdom of Solomon: and behold, a greater than Solomon is here. I am fearful that the men of Nineveh will rise in judgment against this generation, and condemn it; for they repented at the preaching of Jonah; and behold, a greater than Jonah is here. O, you that sit under the gospel's joyful sound, from Sabbath to Sabbath, and you that neglect the means of grace, who know your Lord's will and obey it not! O, you that have exalted to heaven in point of privileges, shall be thrust down to hell; for if the mighty works that have been done in you had been done in Tyra and Sidon, it would have remained unto this day. Wherefore I beseech you, in the name of the Lord Jesus Christ, to repent and quickly put away from among you the evil of your doings, and turn unto the Lord your God with weeping, with mourning, and with fasting. It may be he will repent himself of the evil that he hath determined against you; lest if ye continue to rebel against the word of the Lord, he will arise in his wrath and say: "Because I have called and ye have refused; I have stretched out my hand and no man regarded; I will laugh at your calamities, and mock when your fear cometh; when your fear cometh as a whirlwind, and distress and anguish shall come upon you; then shall ye call, and I will not answer; ye shall seek me early, but ye shall not find me." And O, my Christian friends, you who have been the professed followers of Christ from ten to twenty years, bear with my plainness of speech, I beseech you, and permit me to ask you, in the name of the Lord Jesus Christ, where are the fruits of righteousness that you have brought forth? Where are the souls that have been converted to God through your instrumentality? Where are the men that will give glory to God on account of your good works? Where are those among you that will boldly vindicate the cause of Jesus and him crucified? They that turn many to righteousness shall shine in the kingdom of heaven as the stars forever and ever; while the slothful and negligent shall be bound hand and foot, and cast in outer darkness, where there are weeping and wailing and gnashing of teeth. O, my Christian friends, if we are ever so happy as just to enter within the gates of the holy city—if it were possible, I say—we should mourn throughout the boundless ages of eternity, for having done so little to promote the cause of Christ and the good of souls.

> Broad as the road that leads to death,
> And thousands walk together there;
> But wisdom shows a narrow path,
> With here and there a traveler.

Yes, glory be to God in the highest, there is here and there a faithful one, who is traveling toward Mount Zion, the city of our God.

MEDITATION X.

> The God who built the sky,
> Hath said, and cannot lie,
> "Impenitence must die
> And be damned."

"What shall it profit a man if he gain the whole world and lose his own soul?" dropped from the dying lips of the companion of my youth. O, God, was not my conscience stung with remorse and horror, and was not my soul torn with anguish, and did not my heart bleed when the summons came: "He must die, and not live." Die! O, must he die! Must we part to meet no more! And O, must I be left forlorn and unprotected! Spare hi life, O God, if consistent with thy will, was my cry; if not, make me to say: "Thy will be done." O, my soul, thou hast watched the sick bed of one who was near to thee, even the half of thyself; thou hast heard his dying groans, and seen his restless head turn from side to side in quest of ease; and his dim eye hath he turned upon thee and implored thee for relief. Alas! what could I do? Friends, what were they but miserable comforters? And he had no God to look to! Heart-rending scene! Who can describe it? O, my soul, thou hast wiped the sweat of death from off his cold forehead, and his eyes hast thou seen glazed in death, and those eyes were fixed upon thee! And thine arm supported his expiring form till the spirit extended to God who gave it. O, my soul, forget not that awful scene; forget not that awful moment. Come, all ye that pass by, and see if there is any sorrow like unto my sorrow. And what gratification will it will be to you, my friends, to think that you have been able to be decked in fine linen and purple, and to fare sumptuously every day, if you are not decked in the pure robes of Christ's righteousness? And, friends, what are they in that awful moment, if the eternal God is not your friend and portion? Could many of our departed friends but speak, they would say, fools you may live, but fools you cannot die. Do not as I have done, but improve your precious hours; take care of your immortal souls. But you have the word of God to guide you. Search the Scriptures, for in them you have eternal life. You have the ministers of the gospel to counsel you, to point you to the Lamb of God, which taketh away the sins of the world. Hear ye them. If you will not hearken to them, such are the hardness and obduracy of your hearts that you would not believe, though one arose from the dead and told you of all the joys of heaven or the terrors of hell.

PRAYER.

O, Lord God, when I consider thy heavens the work of thy fingers, the sun, moon, and stars, what is man that thou art mindful of him, or the son of man that thou shouldst visit him? Thou didst at first create man after thine image, pure and upright; but man, by his disobedience, fell from that holy and happy state, and hath involved all his posterity in guilt and ruin. Thine awful sentence was just: "Dust thou art, and unto dust thou

shalt return." Help me to realize that thou art a con-
suming fire to those that obey thee not, and that thou art
arrayed in terrible majesty. Thou chargest thine angels
with folly, and the heavens are not clean in thy sight;
how much more filthy and abominable must be man, who
drinketh in iniquity like water? Thou canst not look
upon the least sin but with abhorrence, and thou wilt by
no means clear the guilty. But though thy name alone
is so terrible, yet Mercy stands pleading at thy bar, saying : Father, I have died ; behold my hands and my side.
Spare them a little longer, and have mercy upon the souls
that thou hast made. O, God, help me to realize that
"man that is born of a woman is of few days, and full of
trouble : he cometh forth as a flower and is cut down ;
yea, man giveth up the ghost, and where is he? And
help me to realize that it is with great tribulation that
we enter through the gates into the holy city. Once
more, I beseech thee, to hear the cry of thy children in
behalf of the unconverted. O, God, this great work is
thine ; thou alone canst perform it. My church and pastor
I recommend to thee. It is all that I can do ; and that
thou wouldst supply them with all needful blessings is
the prayer of thine unworthy handmaiden.

MEDITATION XI.

" Not every one that saith, Lord, Lord, shall enter into
the kingdom of heaven, but he that doeth the will of my
Father which is in heaven. Many will say unto me in
that day, Lord, Lord, have we not prophesied in thy
name, and in thy name cast out devils, and in thy name
done many wonderful works? And then will I profess
unto them I never knew you. Depart from me, ye
workers of iniquity. Blessed is he that doeth the will
of my Father, that he may have right to the tree of life
and may enter through the gates into the holy city ; fo
the kingdom of heaven is like unto a man which sowec
good seed in his field : but whilst men slept the enem!
came, and sowed tares among the wheat. The servan
saith unto him, Sir, didst not thou sow good seed in th;
field ; from whence, then, hath it tares? He sayeth unt
him, An enemy hath done this ; let both grow togethe
until the harvest ; and in time of harvest I will say t
the reapers, Bind the tares in bundles, to burn them.
Many who profess the name of Jesus are not careful t

walk according to their profession, and thereby prove
themselves a stumbling-block and a rock of offense in
the way of sinners ; but when the mighty angel shall descend from heaven, and step one foot upon the earth and
the other upon the sea, and swear by him that liveth for
ever and ever, that time shall be no longer ; when the
last trumpet shall sound, "Awake, ye dead, and come to
judgment ;" when the world shall be on fire, and the ele-
ments shall pass away with a great noise, and the heavens shall be rolled together as a scroll ; when death, and
hell, and the sea shall deliver up the dead that are in
them, and all nations, kindreds, tongues, and people shall
be arrayed before the awful bar of God, and the books
shall be opened ; then, then, if we have not the pure and
undefiled religion of Jesus, wo, wo, wo, will be unto
us ! Better for us that we had never been born ; better
for us that a mill-stone were hanged about our necks,
and that we were cast into the depths of the sea.

MEDITATION XII.

> Come, welcome death, the end of fear,
> I am prepared to die ;
> I trust my soul will straight ascend,
> Up to the Lord on high.

Alas ! and am I born to die ! O, my soul, wilt thou
ere long take thy flight to realms of endless bliss, or to
the shades of darkest night, and leave this frail tenement? Will these eyes be closed, a lump of cold and
lifeless clay ; these lips cease to speak, and this heart
cease to beat ; these hands and feet become inactive,
cold and stiff ; and this form of mine become food for
worms, and turn to dust? Alas ! alas ! how mournful is
the thought ! But, pale messenger, I fear thee not, with
all thy grim and ghastly terrors, for my Redeemer lives.
He lives, and he is able to disarm thee of thy sting ; and
no one is able to pluck me out of my Redeemer's hand.
He will safely carry me through the dark valley and the
shadow of death, and angels will convey me to heaven.
Then, while my body lies mouldering here, my soul shall
rest from all sorrows, and shall chant the praises of my
Redeemer till the last trumpet shall sound ; then shall
my sleeping dust awake, and my soul and body be re-
united, and fly with transport to meet my Saviour, when
he shall come with ten thousand of his saints and angels
to take vengeance on his enemies.

The trumpet sounds,
Hell trembles,
Heaven rejoices;
Lift up your heads, ye saints, with cheerful voices,
No more shall atheist mock his long delay.
His vengeance sleeps no more.
Behold the day!
His guards are nigh;
Tempest and fire attend him down the sky.

When God appears,
All nations shall adore him;
Whilst sinners tremble,
Saints rejoice before him.

PRAYER.

Almighty God, it is the glorious hope of a blessed immortality beyond the grave that supports thy children
through this vale of tears. Forever blessed be thy name,
that thou hast implanted this hope in my bosom. If
thou hast indeed plucked my soul as a brand from the
burning, it is not because thou hast seen any worth in
me; but it is because of thy distinguishing mercy, for
mercy is thy darling attribute, and thou delightest in
mercy, and art not willing that any should perish, but
that all should come to the knowledge of the truth as it
is in Jesus. Clothe my soul with humility as with a
garment. Grant that I may bring forth the fruits of a
meek and quiet spirit. Enable me to adorn the doctrines
of God my Saviour by a well-regulated life and conversation. May I become holy, even as thou art holy, and
pure, even as thou art pure. Bless all my friends and
benefactors—those who have given me a cup of cold
water in thy name, the Lord reward them. Forgive all
my enemies. May I love them that hate me, and pray
for them that despitefully use and persecute me. Preserve me from slanderous tongues, O God, and let not
my good be evil spoken of. Let not a repining thought
enter my heart, nor a murmuring sigh heave from my
bosom; but may I cheerfully bear with all the trials of
life. Clothe me with the pure robes of Christ's righteousness, and that when he shall come in flaming fire to
judge the world, I may appear before him with joy, and
not with grief; and not only for myself do I ask these
blessings, but for all the sons and daughters of Adam,
as thou art no respecter of persons, and as all distinc-
tions wither in the grave. Grant all prejudices and ani-

mosities may cease from among men. May we all realize
that promotion cometh not from the East nor from the
West, but that it is God that putteth up one and setteth
down another. May the rich be rich in faith and good
works toward our Lord Jesus Christ, and may the poor
have an inheritance among the saints in light, a crown
incorruptible that fadeth not away, eternal in the heavens. And now what wait we for? Be pleased to grant
that we may at last join with all the Israel of God in
celebrating thy praise.

MEDITATION XIII.

The widow and the fatherless,
Seek for his aid in sharp distress;
In him the poor and helpless find
A God just as a father kind.

"Leave thy fatherless children, I will preserve them."
And, Lord, thou hast preserved me alive. Whilst thousands as good by nature, and better by practice, have
gone to silence, thine eye hath watched the helpless years
of my infancy and youth, and thou hast preserved me
from thousands of temptations to which I have been exposed. And let thy widows trust in me. Lord, in thee
I have trusted, let me never be confounded.

"Thou shalt by no means afflict any fatherless child:
if thou afflict them, and they cry at all unto me, I will
surely hear their cry." Lord, when mine enemies multi-
plied themselves against me, then I cried unto thee in my
trouble, and thou didst deliver me from all my distresses.
Thou didst behold from thy holy habitation that I was
wrongfully persecuted, and that there was none to help.
Then was thine anger kindled, and thy wrath waxed hot
against mine adversaries, and thine own arm saved me,
and thine own right arm wrought salvation. Thou didst
vindicate my cause in the presence of mine enemies, and
didst bring forth my righteousness to light as the noon-
day. "Let all those be ashamed that wrongfully persecute my soul; that say unto me. ha, ha, where is thy
God?"

Bless the Lord, O my soul, and all that is within me
bless his holy name. Come, magnify the Lord with
me, and let us exalt his name together. I cried unto
him in my trouble, and he delivered me from all my
distresses. Come, all ye that have breath, and I will tell
you what great things the Lord hath done for my soul;

how he hath delivered my feet from the miry clay and the horrible pit, and hath put a new song into my mouth, even praise unto God. What shall I render unto the Lord for all his benefits? I will take the cup of salvation, and will pay my vows before him in the presence of all his people. I will consecrate my soul and body and all the powers of my mind to his service, from this time henceforth; yea, even forever more; for his mercies are more to me than the hairs of my head or the sands upon the sea shore. Trust not in an arm of flesh; for vain is the help of man. Come, all ye poor and needy, ye widows and fatherless, trust in the Lord. He is your help and your shield; for whom he loveth he chasteneth, even as a father the son in whom he delighteth; neither doth he willingly afflict nor grieve the children of men. Although the fig-tree shall not blossom, neither shall fruit be in the vine, yet will I rejoice in the Lord, I will joy in the God of my salvation.

PRAYER.

O Lord God, as the heavens are high above the earth, so are thy ways above our ways, and thy thoughts above our thoughts. For wise and holy purposes best known to thyself, thou hast seen fit to deprive me of all earthly relatives; but when my father and mother forsook me, then thou didst take me up. I desire to thank thee that I am this day a living witness to testify that thou art a God that will ever vindicate the cause of the poor and needy, and that thou hast always proved thyself to be a friend and father to me. O, continue thy loving kindness, even unto the end; and when health and strength begin to decay, and I, as it were, draw nigh unto the grave, O then afford me thy heart-cheering presence, and enable me to rely entirely upon thee. Never leave me nor forsake me, but have mercy upon me for thy great name's sake. And not for myself alone do I ask these blessings, but for all the poor and needy, all widows and fatherless children, and for the stranger in distress; and may they call upon thee in such a manner as to be convinced that thou art a prayer-hearing and prayer-answering God; and thine shall be the praise forever. Amen.

> Prayer is the Christian's vital breath,
> The Christian's native air;
> His watch-word at the gate of death,
> He enters heaven with prayer.

MEDITATION XIV.

If there's an idol in my heart,
Whate'er that idol be ;
Help me to tear it from thy throne,
And worship only thee.

"And he gave them their request, but he sent leanness into their souls." O, my soul, has not the voice of thy weeping ascended up before the throne of God? Hast thou not almost offended the majesty of heaven with thy murmurings? Hast thou not wept like the rebellious Israelites for the onions and the garlics that were in Egypt? And hast thou not rejected the Lord from reigning king over thee? O, my soul, are not thine affections prone to wander from the fountain of living waters, and to place themselves upon broken cisterns, that can hold no water? Parent of mercies, rivet this heart alone upon thyself. Help me truly to say, whom have I in heaven but thee? and there is none upon the earth that I desire beside thee. O, my soul, cast off from thee every darling sin, however dear, even to the plucking out of a right eye or the cutting off a right hand. Soon this mortal will put on immortality, and this corruption incorruption, and these eyes will open upon eternal scenes ; then, O, my soul, what gratification will it be to thee that all the desires of thine heart were given thee. As death leaves me, so judgment will find me. O, my soul, vain and trifling will then appear thy disappointments. Cleanse thou me, O God, from secret faults. O, my Father, strip this poor unworthy worm of thine from every impure and unholy desire ; from all self-righteousness, pride, and hypocrisy ; from slander and deceit. Hast thou not a blessing for me? Bless me, even me, O my Father! Bless me when I go out and when I come in ; when I lie down and when I rise up. Put underneath me thine everlasting arms, and keep me from all evil. Sooner extinguish the lamp of life than leave me to bring a reproach upon thy cause, or wound the hearts of thy children. Hold me in the hollow of thine hand or I shall fall. Lord, save me, or I perish. Mind filled with gloomy doubts and fears ; feel at times as though I should fear to die. Death is truly the king of terrors. O, my Saviour, take from me this awful fear, I humbly beseech thee ; and when I come upon the bed of sickness, do thou be graciously pleased to manifest thyself unto me, and enable me to lean my head upon thy bosom. Let guardian angels watch around my pillow; and when I behold my weeping friends, may I say to them with a cheerful smile, weep not for me, but weep for yourselves and for your children. And when pain and anguish shall distort these features, may I calmly say, did Jesus thus suffer, and shall I repine? O, death, where is thy sting? O, grave, where is thy victory? May this poor unworthy worm of thine be clothed with the breast-plate of righteousness, and girded with the helmet of salvation. May the testimony of Jesus be within her, his seal engraved upon her forehead, and her name written in the Lamb's book of life. May she overcome the temptations of the wicked one, and wash her robes white in the blood of the Lamb; and do thou present her faultless before the Father's throne, without spot or wrinkle or any such thing; and when thou shalt call me to go, may I arise, having my lamps trimmed and burning, not having a wish or a desire to stay, but to depart and dwell with thee, which is far better. Blessed is that servant whom his Lord, when he cometh, shall find watching.

LECTURE.

DELIVERED AT THE FRANKLIN HALL, BOSTON, SEPTEM-
BER 21, 1832.

Why sit ye here and die? If we say we will go to a
foreign land, the famine and the pestilence are there, and
there we shall die. If we sit here, we shall die. Come,
let us plead our cause before the whites. If they save
us alive. we shall live ; and if they kill us, we shall but die.

Methinks I heard a spiritual interrogation—"Who shall
go forward and take off the reproach that is cast upon
the people of color? Shall it be a woman?" And my
heart made this reply : "If it is Thy will, be it even so,
Lord Jesus !"

I have heard much respecting the horrors of slavery ;
but may heaven forbid that the generality of my color
throughout these United States should experience any
more of its horrors than to be a servant of servants, or
hewers of wood and drawers of water ! Tell us no more
of Southern slavery ; for, with few exceptions, although
I may be very erroneous in my opinion, yet I consider
our condition but little better than that. Yet, after all,
methinks there are no chains so galling as the chains of
ignorance—no fetters so binding as those that bind the
soul, and exclude it from the vast field of usefulness and
scientific knowledge. O, had I received the advantages
of early education, my idea would, ere now, have ex-
panded far and wide ; but, alas ! I possess nothing but
moral capability—no teaching but the teaching of the
Holy Spirit.

I have asked several individuals of my sex, who trans-
act business for themselves, if, providing our girls were
to give them the most satisfactory references, they would
not be willing to grant them an equal opportunity with
others? Their reply has been : For their own part, they
had no objection ; but as it was not the custom, were
they to take them into their employ, they would be in
danger of losing the public patronage.

And such is the powerful force of prejudice. Let our
girls possess what amiable qualities of soul they may ;

let their characters be fair and spotless as innocence itself; let their natural taste and ingenuity be what they may, it is impossible for scarce an individual of them to rise above the condition of servants. Ah! why is this cruel and unfeeling distinction? Is it merely because God has made our complexion to vary? If it be, O shame to soft, relenting humanity! "Tell it not in Gath! publish it not in the streets of Askelon!" Yet, after all, methinks were the American free people of color to turn their attention more assiduously to moral worth and intellectual improvements, this would be the result: Prejudice would gradually diminish, and the whites would be compelled to say, unloose those fetters!

> Though black their skins as shades of night,
> Their hearts are pure, their souls are white.

Few white persons of either sex, who are calculated for anything else, are willing to spend their lives and bury their talents in performing mean, servile labor. And such is the horrible idea that I entertain respecting a life of servitude, that if I conceived of there being no possibility of my rising above the condition of a servant, I would gladly hail death as a welcome messenger. O, horrible idea, indeed, to possess noble souls, aspiring after high and honorable acquirements, yet confined by the chains of ignorance and poverty to lives of continual drudgery and toil. Neither do I know of any who have enriched themselves by spending their lives as house-domestics, washing windows, shaking carpets, brushing boots, or tending upon gentlemen's tables. I can but die for expressing my sentiments; and I am as willing to die by the sword as the pestilence; for I am a true-born American; your blood flows in my veins, and your spirit fires my breast.

I observed a piece in the *Liberator* a few months since, stating that the colonizationists had published a work respecting us, asserting that we were lazy and idle. I confute them on that point. Take us generally as a people, we are neither lazy nor idle; and considering how little we have to excite or stimulate us, I am almost astonished that there are so many industrious and ambitious ones to be found: although I acknowledge, with extreme sorrow, that there are some who never were and never will be serviceable to society. And have you not a similar class among yourselves?

Again. It was asserted that we were a "ragged set, crying for liberty." I reply to it : The whites have so long and so loudly proclaimed the theme of equal rights and privileges, that our souls have caught the flame also, ragged as we are. As far as our merit deserves, we feel a common desire to rise above the condition of servants and drudges. I have learned, by bitter experience, that continual hard labor deadens the energies of the soul, and benumbs the faculties of the mind ; the ideas become confined, the mind barren, and, like the scorching sands of Arabia, produces nothing ; or, like the uncultivated soil, brings forth thorns and thistles.

Again. Continual hard labor irritates our tempers and sours our dispositions ; the whole system becomes worn out with toil and fatigue ; nature herself becomes almost exhausted, and we care but little whether we live or die. It is true, that the free people of color throughout these United States are neither bought nor sold, nor under the lash of the cruel driver. Many obtain a comfortable support ; but few, if any, have an opportunity of becoming rich and independent ; and the employments we must pursue are as unprofitable to us as the spider's web or the floating bubbles that vanish into air. As servants, we are respected ; but let us presume to aspire any higher, our employer regards us no longer. And were it not that the King Eternal has declared that Ethiopia shall stretch forth her hands unto God, I should indeed despair.

I do not consider it derogatory, my friends. for persons to live out to service. There are many whose inclination leads them to aspire no higher ; and I would highly commend the performance of almost anything for an honest livelihood ; but where constitutional strength is wanting, labor of this kind, in its mildest form, is painful ; and, doubtless, many are the prayers that have ascended to heaven from Afric's daughters for strength to perform their work. O, many are the tears that have been shed for the want of that strength ! Most of our color have dragged out a miserable existence of servitude from the cradle to the grave. And what literary acquirements can be made, or useful knowledge derived, from either maps, books, or charts. by those who continually drudge from Monday morning until Sunday noon? O, ye fairer sisters, whose hands are never soiled, whose nerves and muscles are never strained, go learn

3*

by experience! Had we had the opportunity that you have had to improve our moral and mental faculties, what would have hindered our intellects from being as bright, and our manners from being as dignified, as yours? Had it been our lot to have been nursed in the lap of affluence and ease, and to have basked beneath the smiles and sunshine of fortune, should we not have naturally supposed that we were never made to toil? And why are not our forms as delicate and our constitutions as slender as yours? Is not the workmanship as curious and complete? Have pity upon us, have pity upon us, O ye who have hearts to feel for other's woes; for the hand of God has touched us. Owing to the disadvantages under which we labor, there are many flowers among us that are

"—— born to bloom unseen,
And waste their fragrance on the desert air."

My beloved brethren, as Christ has died in vain for those who will not accept of offered mercy, so will it be vain for the advocates of freedom to spend their breath in our behalf, unless with united hearts and souls you make some mighty efforts to raise your sons and daughters from the horrible state of servitude and degradation in which they are placed. It is upon you that woman depends; she can do but little beside using her influence; and it is for her sake and yours that I have come forward and made myself a hissing and a reproach among the people; for I am also one of the wretched and miserable daughters of the descendants of Africa. Do you ask: "Why are you wretched and miserable?" I reply: Look at many of the most worthy and interesting of us doomed to spend our lives in gentlemen's kitchens. Look at our young men—smart, active and energetic, with souls filled with ambitious fire; if they look forward, alas! what are their prospects? They can be nothing but the humblest laborer, on account of their dark complexion; hence many of them lose their ambition, and become worthless. Look at our middle-aged men, clad in their rusty plaids and coats. In winter, every cent they earn goes to buy their wood and pay their rent; their poor wives also toil beyond their strength, to help support their families. Look at our aged sires, whose heads are whitened with the frosts of seventy winters, with their old wood-saws on their backs. Alas, what keeps us so? Prejudice, ignorance, and poverty. But ah! methinks our oppression is soon to come to an end; yea, before the Majesty of heaven our groans and cries have reached the ears of the Lord of Sabaoth. As the prayers and tears of Christians will avail the finally impenitent nothing, neither will the prayers and tears of the friends of humanity avail us anything unless we possess a spirit of virtuous emulation within our breasts. Did the pilgrims, when they first landed on these shores, quietly compose themselves, and say: "The Britons have all the money and all the power, and we must continue their servants forever?" Did they sluggishly sigh, and say: "Our lot is hard; the Indians own the soil, and we cannot cultivate it?" No; they first made powerful efforts to raise themselves, and then God raised up those illustrious patriots, WASHINGTON and LAFAYETTE, to assist and defend them. And, my brethren, have you made a powerful effort? Have you prayed the Legislature for mercy's sake to grant you all the rights and privileges of free citizens, that your daughters may rise to that degree of respectability which true merit deserves, and your sons above the servile situations which most of them fill?

AN ADDRESS.

The frowns of the world shall never discourage me,
nor its smiles flatter me ; for. with the help of God, I am
resolved to withstand the fiery darts of the devil and the
assaults of wicked men.   The righteous are as bold as a
lion, but the wicked fleeth when no man pursueth.   I fear
neither men nor devils ; for the God in whom I trust is
able to deliver me from the rage and malice of my enemies, and from them that rise up against me.   The only
motive that has prompted me to raise my voice in your
behalf, my friends, is because I have discovered that religion is held in low repute among some of us ; and
purely to promote the cause of Christ, and the good of
souls, in the hope that others more experienced. more
able and talented than myself, might go forward and do
likewise.   I expect to render a strict. a solemn, and an
awful account to God for the motives that have prompted
me to exertion, and for those with which I shall address
you this evening.

What I have to say concerns the whole of us as Christians and as people ; and if you will be so kind as to
give me a hearing this once, you shall receive the incense
of a grateful heart.

The day is coming, my friends, and I rejoice in that
day, when the secrets of all hearts shall be manifested
before saints and angels, men and devils,   It will be a
great day of joy and rejoicing to the humble followers of
Christ, but a day of terror and dismay to hypocrites and
unbelievers.   Of that day and hour knoweth no man ; no,
not even the angels in heaven, but the Father only.   The
dead that are in Christ shall be raised first.   Blessed is
he that shall have a part in the first resurrection.   Ah !
methinks I hear the finally impenitent cry : "Rocks and
mountains, fall upon us and hide us from the wrath of
the Lamb, and from him that sitteth upon the throne."

High on a cloud our God shall come,
Bright thrones prepare his way ;
Thunder and darkness. fire and storm,
Lead on the dreadful day.

Christ shall descend in the clouds of heaven, surrounded by ten thousand of his saints and angels, and it shall be very tempestuous round about him; and before him shall be gathered all nations and kindred and tongues and people; and every knee shall bow and every tongue confess. They also that pierced him shall look upon him and mourn. Then shall the king separate the righteous from the wicked, as a shepherd divideth the sheep from the goats, and shall place the righteous on his right hand and the wicked upon his left. Then, says Christ, shall be weeping and wailing and gnashing of teeth, when ye shall see Abraham and the prophets sitting in the kingdom of heaven, and ye yourselves thrust out. Then shall the righteous shine forth in the kingdom of their Father as the sun. He that hath ears to hear, let him hear. The poor, despised followers of Christ will not then regret their sufferings here; they shall be carried by angels into Abraham's bosom, and shall be comforted; and the Lord God shall wipe away their tears. You will then be convinced before the assembled multitudes whether they strove to promote the cause of Christ or whether they sought for gain or applause, "Strive to enter at the straight gate; for many, I say unto you, shall seek to enter in and shall not be able. For except your righteousness shall exceed the righteousness of the Scribes and Pharisees, ye shall in no wise enter into the kingdom of heaven."

Ah! methinks I see this people lying in wickedness; and as the Lord liveth, and as your souls live, were it not for the few righteous that are to be found among us, we should become as Sodom, and like unto Gomorrah. Christians have too long slumbered and slept. Sinners stumbled into hell, and still are stumbling, for the want of Christian exertion; and the devil is going about like a roaring lion seeking whom he may devour. And I make bold to say that many who profess the name of Christ at the present day, live so widely different from what becometh the gospel of our Lord Jesus Christ, that they cannot and they dare not reason to the world upon righteousness and judgment to come.

Be not offended because I tell you the truth; for I believe that God has fired my soul with a holy zeal for his cause. It was God alone who inspired my heart to publish the meditations thereof; and it was done with pure motives of love to your souls, in the hope that Christians might examine themselves, and sinners become pricked in their hearts. It is the word of God, though men and devils may oppose it. It is the word of God, and little did I think that any of the professed followers of Christ would have frowned upon me and discouraged and hindered its progress.

Ah, my friends, I am speaking as one who expects to give account at the bar of God; I am speaking as a dying mortal to dying mortals. I fear there are many who have named the name of Jesus at the present day that strain at a gnat and swallow a camel. They neither enter into the kingdom of heaven themselves nor suffer others to enter in. They would pull the motes out of their brother's eye when they have a beam in their own eye. And were our blessed Lord and Saviour Jesus Christ upon the earth, I believe he would say of many that are called by his name: "O, ye hypocrites, ye generation of vipers, how can you escape the damnation of hell." I have enlisted in the holy warfare, and Jesus is my Captain; and the Lord's battle I mean to fight until my voice expire in death. I expect to be hated of all men, and persecuted even unto death, for righteousness and the truth's sake.

A few remarks upon moral subjects, and I close. I am a strong advocate for the cause of God and for the cause of freedom. I am not your enemy, but a friend both to you and your children. Suffer me, then, to express my sentiments but this once, however severe they may appear to be, and then hereafter let me sink into oblivion, and let my name die in forgetfulness.

Had the ministers of the gospel shunned the very appearance of evil; had they faithfully discharged their duty, whether we would have heard them or not, we should have been a very different people from what we now are; but they have kept the truth, as it were, hid from our eyes, and have cried: "Peace! peace!" when there was no peace. They have plastered us up with untempered mortar, and have been, as it were, blind leaders of the blind.

It appears to me that there are no people under the heavens so unkind and so unfeeling toward their own as are the descendants of fallen Africa. I have been something of a traveler in my day; and the general cry among the people is, "Our own color are the greatest opposers ;' and even the whites say that we are greater enemies toward each other than they are toward us. Shall we be a hissing and a reproach among the nations of the earth any longer? Shall they laugh us to scorn forever? ·We might become a highly respectable people ; respectable we now consider ourselves, but we might become a highly distinguished and intelligent people. And how ? In convincing the world by our own efforts, however feeble, that nothing is wanting on our part but opportunity. Without these efforts we shall never be a people, nor our descendants after us.

But God has said that Ethiopia shall stretch forth her hands unto him. True, but God uses means to bring about his purposes ; and unless the rising generation manifest a different temper and disposition toward each other from what we have manifested, the generation following will never be an enlightened people. We this day are considered as one of the most degraded races upon the face of the earth. It is useless for us any longer to sit with our hands folded reproaching the whites, for that will never elevate us. All the nations of the earth have distinguished themselves, and have shown forth a noble and a gallant spirit. Look at the suffering Greeks. Their proud souls revolted at the idea of serving a tyrannical nation who were no better than themselves, and perhaps not so good. They made a mighty effort and arose ; their souls were knit together in the holy bonds of love and union ; they were united, and came off victorious. Look at the French in the late rebellion ; no traitors among them to expose their plans to the crowned heads of Europe. "Liberty or death" was their cry. And the Haytians, though they have not been acknowledged as a nation, yet their firmness of character and independence of spirit have been greatly admired and highly applauded. Look at the Poles, a feeble people. They arose against three hundred thousand mighty men of Russia : and though they did not gain the conquest, yet they obtained the name of gallant Poles. And even the wild Indians of the forest are more united than ourselves. Insult one of them and you insult a thousand. They also have contended for their rights and privileges, and are held in higher repute than we are.

And why is it, my friends, that we are despised above

all the nations upon the earth? Is it merely because our skins are tinged with a sable hue? No, nor will I ever believe that it is. What then is it? O, it is because we and our fathers have dealt treacherously one with another, and because many of us now possess that envious and malicious disposition that we had rather die than see each other rise an inch above a beggar. No gentle methods are used to promote love and friendship among us, but much is done to destroy it. Shall we be a hissing and a reproach among the nations of the earth any longer? Shall they laugh us to scorn forever?

Ingratitude is one of the worst passions that reigns in the human breast. It is this that cuts the tender fibres of the soul; for it is impossible for us to love those who are ungrateful toward us. "Behold," says that wise man, Solomon, counting one by one, "a man have I found in a thousand, but a woman among all those have I not found."

I have sometimes thought that God had almost departed from among us. And why? Because Christ has said if we say we love the Father and hate our brother, we are liars, and the truth is not in us; and certainly if we were the true followers of Christ, I think we could not show such a disposition toward each other as we do, for God is all love.

Finally I have exerted myself both for your temporal and eternal welfare as far as I am able; and my soul has been so discouraged within me that I have almost been induced to exclaim: "Would to God that my tongue hereafter might cleave to the roof of my mouth and become silent forever;" and then I have felt that the Christian has no time to be idle, and I must be active, knowing that the night of death cometh, in which no man can work. And my mind has become raised to such an extent that I will willingly die for the cause that I have espoused; for I cannot die in a more glorious cause than in the defense of God and his laws.

O, woman, woman, upon you I call; for upon your exertions almost entirely depends whether the rising generation shall be anything more than we have been or not. O, woman, woman, your example is powerful, your influence great; it extends over your husbands and over your children, and throughout the circle of your acquaintance. Then let me exhort you to cultivate among yourselves spirit of Christian love and unity, having charity one for

another. without which all our goodness is as sounding
brass and as a tinkling cymbal. And, O my God, I beseech thee to grant that the nations of the earth may hiss
at us no longer. O, suffer them not to laugh us to scorn
forever.

AN ADDRESS.

DELIVERED AT THE AFRICAN MASONIC HALL, BOSTON, FEBRUARY 27, 1833.

African rights and liberty is a subject that ought to fire the breast of every free man of color in these United States, and excite in his bosom a lively, deep, decided, and heart-felt interest. When I cast my eyes on the long list of illustrious names that are enrolled on the bright annals of fame among the whites, I turn my eyes within and ask my thoughts, "Where are the names of *our* illustrious ones?" It must certainly have been for the want of energy on the part of the free people of color that they have been long willing to bear the yoke of oppression. It must have been the want of ambition and force that has given the whites occasion to say that our natural abilities are not as good, and our capacities by nature inferior to theirs. They boldly assert that did we possess a natural independence of soul, and feel a love for liberty within our breasts, some one of our sable race, long before this, would have testified it, notwithstanding the disadvantages under which we labor. We have made ourselves appear altogether unqualified to speak in our own defense, and are therefore looked upon as objects of pity and commiseration. We have been imposed upon, insulted, and derided on every side; and now, if we complain, it is considered as the height of impertinence. We have suffered ourselves to be considered as dastards, cowards, mean, faint-hearted wretches; and on this account (not because of our complexion) many despise us, and would gladly spurn us from their presence.

These things have fired my soul with a holy indignation, and compelled me thus to come forward and endeavor to turn their attention to knowledge and improvement, for knowledge is power. I would ask, is it blindness of mind or stupidity of soul or the want of education that has caused our men who are sixty or seventy years of age never to let their voices be heard nor their hands be raised in behalf of their color? Or has it been for fear of offend-

ing the whites? If it has, O ye fearful ones, throw off
your fearfulness and come forth, in the name of the Lord
and in the strength of the God of Justice, and make yourselves useful and active members in society; for they
admire a noble and patriotic spirit in others, and should
they not admire it in us? If you are men, convince them
that you possess the spirit of men; and as your day so
shall your strength be. Have the sons of Africa no souls?
Feel they no ambitious desires? Shall the chains of ignorance forever confine them? Shall the insipid appella-
tion of "clever negroes" or "good creatures" any longer
content them? Where can we find among ourselves the
man of science, or a philosopher, or an able statesman,
or a counsellor at law? Show me our fearless and brave,
our noble and gallant ones. Where are our lecturers on
natural history and our critics in useful knowledge?
There may be a few such men among us, but they are
rare. It is true, our fathers bled and died in the revolu-
tionary war, and others fought bravely, under the com-
mand of Jackson, in defense of liberty. But where is
the man that has distinguished himself in these modern
days by acting wholly in the defense of African rights
and liberty? There was one; although he sleeps, his
memory lives.

I am sensible that there are many highly intelligent
gentlemen of color in these United States in the force of
whose arguments, doubtless, I should discover my infe-
riority; but if they are blessed with wit and talent, friends
and fortune, why have they not made themselves men of
eminence by striving to take all the reproach that is cast
upon the people of color, and in endeavoring to alleviate
the woes of their brethren in bondage? Talk, without
effort, is nothing. You are abundantly capable, gentlemen, of making yourselves men of distinction; and this
gross neglect on your part causes my blood to boil within
me. Here is the grand cause which hinders the rise and
progress of the people of color. It is the want of laudable
ambition and requisite courage.

Individuals have been distinguished according to their
genius and talents ever since the first formation of man,
and will continue to be while the world stands. The
different grades rise to honor and respectability as their
merits may deserve. History informs us that we sprung
from one of the most learned nations of the whole earth;

from the seat, if not the parent of science ; yes, poor, despised Africa was once the resort of sages and legislators of other nations, was esteemed the school of learning, and the most illustrious men of Greece flocked thither for instruction. But it was our gross sins and abominations that provoked the Almighty to frown thus heavily upon us and give our glory unto others. Sin and prodigality have caused the downfall of nations, kings, and emperors ; and were it not that God in wrath remembers mercy, we might indeed despair ; but a promise is left us : " Ethiopia shall again stretch forth her hands unto God."

But it is no use for us to boast that we sprung from this learned and enlightened nation, for this day a thick mist of moral gloom hangs over millions of our race. Our condition as a people has been low for hundreds of years, and it will continue to be so, unless, by true piety and virtue, we strive to regain that which we have lost. White Americans, by their prudence, economy, and exertions, have sprung up and become one of the most flourishing nations in the world, distinguished for their knowledge of the arts and sciences, for their polite literature. While our minds are vacant and starving for want of knowledge, theirs are filled to overflowing. Most of our color have been taught to stand in fear of the white man from their earliest infancy, to work as soon as they could walk, and to call "master" before they scarce could lisp the name of *mother*. Continual fear and laborious servitude have in some degree lessened in us that natural force and energy which belong to man ; or else, in defiance of opposition, our men, before this, would have nobly and boldly contended for their rights. But give the man of color an equal opportunity with the white from the cradle to manhood, and from manhood to the grave, and you would discover the dignified statesman, the man of science, and the philosopher. But there is no such opportunity for the sons of Africa, and I fear that our powerful ones are fully determined that there never shall be. Forbid, ye Powers on high, that it should any longer be said that our men possess no force. O ye sons of Africa, when will your voices be heard in our legislative halls, in defiance of your enemies, contending for equal rights and liberty ? How can you, when you reflect from what you have fallen, refrain from crying mightily unto God, to turn away from us the fierceness of his anger, and remember our transgres-ions against us no more forever. But a God of infinite purity will not regard the prayers of those who hold religion in one hand, and prejudice, sin, and pollution in the other; he will not regard the prayers of self-righteousness and hypocrisy. Is it possible, I exclaim, that for the want of knowledge we have labored for hundreds of years to support others, and been content to receive what they chose to give us in return? Cast your eyes about, look as far as you can see; all, all is owned by the lordly white, except here and there a lowly dwelling which the man of color, midst deprivations, fraud, and opposition has been scarce able to procure. Like King Solomon, who put neither nail nor hammer to the temple, yet received the praise; so also have the white Americans gained themselves a name, like the names of the great men that are in the earth. while in reality we have been their principal foundation and support. We have pursued the shadow, they have obtained the substance; we have performed the labor, they have received the profits; we have planted the vines, they have eaten the fruits of them.

I would implore our men, and especially our rising youth, to flee from the gambling board and the dance-hall; for we are poor, and have no money to throw away. I do not consider dancing as criminal in itself, but it is astonishing to me that our young men are so blind to their own interest and the future welfare of their children as to spend their hard earnings for this frivolous amusement; for it has been carried on among us to such an unbecoming extent that it has become absolutely disgusting. "Faithful are the wounds of a friend, but the kisses of an enemy are deceitful." Had those men among us, who have had an opportunity, turned their attention as assiduously to mental and moral improvement as they have to gambling and dancing, I might have remained quietly at home and they stood contending in my place. These polite accomplishments will never enroll your names on the bright annals of fame who admire the belle void of intellectual knowledge, or applaud the dandy that talks largely on politics, without striving to assist his fellow in the revolution, when the nerves and muscles of every other man forced him into the field of action. You have a right to rejoice, and to let your hearts cheer you in the days of your youth; yet remember that for all these things God will bring you into judgment. Then, O ye sons of Africa, turn your mind from these perishable objects, and contend for the cause of God and the rights of man. Form yourselves into temperance societies. There are temperate men among you; then why will you any longer neglect to strive, by your example, to suppress vice in all its abhorrent forms? You have been told repeatedly of the glorious results arising from temperance, and can you bear to see the whites arising in honor and respectability without endeavoring to grasp after that honor and respectability also?

But I forbear. Let our money, instead of being thrown away as heretofore, be appropriated for schools and seminaries of learning for our children and youth. We ought to follow the example of the whites in this respect. Nothing would raise our respectability, add to our peace and happiness, and reflect so much honor upon us, as to be ourselves the promoters of temperance, and the supporters, as far as we are able, of useful and scientific knowledge. The rays of light and knowledge have been hid from our view; we have been taught to consider ourselves as scarce superior to the brute creation; and have performed the most laborious part of American drudgery. Had we as a people received one-half the early advantages the whites have received, I would defy the Government of these United States to deprive us any longer of our rights.

I am informed that the agent of the Colonization Society has recently formed an association of young men for the purpose of influencing those of us to go to Liberia who may feel disposed. The colonizationists are blind to their own interest, for should the nations of the earth make war with America, they would find their forces much weakened by our absence; or should we remain here, can our "brave soldiers" and "fellow-citizens," as they were termed in time of calamity, condescend to defend the rights of the whites and be again deprived of their own, or sent to Liberia in return? Or, if the colonizationists are the real friends to Africa, let them expend the money which they collect, in erecting a college to educate her injured sons in this land of gospel, light, and liberty; for it would be most thankfully received on our part, and convince us of the truth of their professions.

and save time, expense, and anxiety. Let them place before us noble objects worthy of pursuit, and see if we prove ourselves to be those unambitious negroes they term us. But, ah, bethinks their hearts are so frozen toward us they had rather their money should be sunk in the ocean than to administer it to our relief; and I fear, if they dared, like Pharaoh, king of Egypt, they would order every male child among us to be drowned. But the most high God is still as able to subdue the lofty pride of these white Americans as He was the heart of that ancient rebel. They say, though we are looked upon as *things*, yet we sprang from a scientific people. Had our men the requisite force and energy they would soon convince them by their efforts, both in public and private, that they were men, or things in the shape of men. Well may the colonizationists laugh us to scorn for our negligence; well may they cry: "Shame to the sons of Africa." As the burden of the Israelites was too great for Moses to bear, so also is our burden too great for our noble advocate to bear. You must feel interested, my brethren, in what he undertakes, and hold up his hands by your good works, or in spite of himself his soul will become discouraged and his heart will die within him; for he has, as it were, the strong bulls of Bashan to contend with.

It is of no use for us to wait any longer for a generation of well educated men to arise. We have slumbered and slept too long already; the day is far spent; the night of death approaches; and you have sound sense and good judgment sufficient to begin with, if you feel disposed to make a right use of it. Let every man of color throughout the United States, who possesses the spirit and principles of a man, sign a petition to Congress to abolish slavery in the District of Columbia, and grant you the rights and privileges of common free citizens; for if you had had faith as a grain of mustard seed, long before this the mountains of prejudice might have been removed. We are all sensible that the Anti-Slavery Society has taken hold of the arm of our whole population, in order to raise them out of the mire. Now all we have to do is, by a spirit of virtuous ambition, to strive to raise ourselves; and I am happy to have it in my power thus publicly to say that the colored inhabitants of this city, in some respects, are beginning to improve. Had the free people of color in these United States nobly and boldly contended for their rights, and showed a natural genius and talent, although not so brilliant as some; had they held up, encouraged and patronized each other, nothing could have hindered us from being a thriving and flourishing people. There has been a fault among us. The reason why our distinguished men have not made themselves more influential, is because they fear that the strong current of opposition through which they must pass would cause their downfall and prove their overthrow. And what gives rise to this opposition? Envy. And what has it amounted to? Nothing. And who are the cause of it? Our whited sepulchres, who want to be great, and don't know how; who love to be called of men "Rabbi, Rabbi;" who put on false sanctity, and humble themselves to their brethren for the sake of acquiring the highest place in the synagogue and the uppermost seat at the feast. You, dearly beloved, who are the genuine followers of our Lord Jesus Christ—the salt of the earth, and the light of the world—are not so culpable. As I told you in the very first of my writing, I tell you again, I am but as a drop in the bucket—as one particle of the small dust of the earth. God will surely raise up those among us who will plead the cause of virtue and the pure principles of morality more eloquently than I am able to do.

It appears to me that America has become like the great City of Babylon, for she has boasted in her heart: "I sit a queen, and am no widow, and shall see no sorrow!" She is, indeed, a seller of slaves and the souls of men; she has made the Africans drunk with the wine of her fornication; she has put them completely beneath her feet, and she means to keep them there; her right hand supports the reins of government and her left hand the wheel of power, and she is determined not to let go her grasp. But many powerful sons and daughters of Africa will shortly arise, who will put down vice and immorality among us, and declare by Him that sitteth upon the throne that they will have their rights; and if refused, I am afraid they will spread horror and devastation around. I believe that the oppression of injured Africa has come up before the Majesty of Heaven; and when our cries shall have reached the ears of the Most High, it will be a tremendous day for the people of this land; for strong is the arm of the Lord God Almighty. Life has almost lost its charms for me; death has lost its sting, and the grave its terrors; and at times I have a strong desire to depart and dwell with Christ, which is far better. Let me entreat my white brethren to awake and save our sons from dissipation and our daughters from ruin. Lend the hand of assistance to feeble merit; plead the cause of virtue among our sable race; so shall our curses upon you be turned into blessings; and though you should endeavor to drive us from these shores, still we will cling to you the more firmly; nor will we attempt to rise above you; we will presume to be called your equals only.

The unfriendly whites first drove the native American from his much loved home. Then they stole our fathers from their peaceful and quiet dwellings, and brought them hither, and made bond-men and bond-women of them and their little ones. They have obliged our brethren to labor; kept them in utter ignorance; nourished them in vice, and raised them in degradation; and now that we have enriched their soil, and filled their coffers, they say that we are not capable of becoming like white men, and that we never can rise to respectability in this country. They would drive us to a strange land. But before I go, the bayonet shall pierce me through. African rights and liberty is a subject that ought to fire the breast of every free man of color in these United States, and excite in his bosom a lively, deep, decided, and heartfelt interest.

4

MRS. STEWART'S

FAREWELL ADDRESS TO HER FRIENDS IN THE CITY OF
BOSTON. DELIVERED SEPTEMBER 21, 1833.

> " Is this vile world a friend to grace,
> To help me on to God?"

Ah, no! for it is with great tribulation that any shall
enter through the gates into the holy city.

My Respected Friends: You have heard me observe
that the shortness of time, the certainty of death, and
the instability of all things here, induced me to turn my
thoughts from earth to heaven. Borne down with a heavy
load of sin and shame, my conscience filled with remorse. Considering the throne of God forever guiltless,
and my own eternal condemnation as just, I was at last
brought to accept of salvation as a free gift, in and
through the merits of a crucified Redeemer. Here I
was brought to see—

> " 'Tis not by works of righteousness
> That our own hands have done;
> But we are saved by grace alone,
> Abounding through the Son."

After these convictions, in imagination I found myself
sitting at the feet of Jesus, clothed in my right mind.
For I before had been like a ship tossed to and fro in a
storm at sea. Then was I glad when I realized the dangers I had escaped ; and then I consecrated my soul and
body, and all the powers of my mind to his service, from
that time henceforth; yea, even for evermore. Amen.

I found that religion was full of benevolence ; I found
there was joy and peace in believing, and I felt as though
I was commanded to come out from the world and be
separate ; to go forward and be baptized. Methought I
heard a spiritual interrogation : "Are you able to drink
of that cup that I have drank of? and to be baptized
with the baptism that I have been baptized with? And
my heart made this reply : Yea, Lord, I am able. Yet
amid these bright hopes I was filled with apprehensive
fears, lest they were false. I found that sin still lurked
within ; it was hard for me to renounce all for Christ,

when I saw my earthly prospects blasted. O, how bitter was that cup. Yet I drank it to its very dregs. It was hard for me to say, Thy will be done; yet I was made to bend and kiss the rod. I was at last made willing to be anything or nothing for my Redeemer's sake. Like many, I was anxious to retain the world in one hand and religion in the other. "Ye cannot serve God and mammon," sounded in my ear, and with giant strength I cut off my right hand, as it were, and plucked out my right eye, and cast them from me, thinking it better to enter life halt and maimed rather than have two hands or eyes to be cast into hell. Thus ended these mighty conflicts, and I received this heart-cheering promise: "That neither death, nor life, nor principalities, nor powers, nor things present, nor things to come should be able to separate me from the love of Christ Jesus our Lord."

And truly, I can say with St. Paul, that at my conversion I came to the people in the fullness of the gospel of grace. Having spent a few months in the city of —— previously, I saw the flourishing condition of their churches and the progress they were making in their Sabbath schools. I visited their Bible classes and heard of the union that existed in their female associations. On my arrival here, not finding scarce an individual who felt interested in these subjects, and but few of the whites, except Mr. Garrison and his friend, Mr. Knap; and hearing that those gentlemen had observed that female influence was powerful, my soul became fired with a holy zeal for your cause; every nerve and muscle in me was engaged in your behalf. I felt that I had a great work to perform, and was in haste to make a profession of my faith in Christ that I might be about my Father's business. Soon after I made this profession the Spirit of God came before me, and I spake before many. When going home, reflecting on what I had said, I felt ashamed, and knew not where I should hide myself. A something said within my breast, "press forward, I will be with thee." And my heart made this reply: "Lord, if thou wilt be with me, then will I speak for thee so long as I live." And thus far I have every reason to believe that it is the divine influence of the Holy Spirit operating upon my heart that could possibly induce me to make the feeble and unworthy efforts that I have.

But to begin my subject. "Ye have heard that it hath

been said whoso is angry with his brother without cause, shall be in danger of the judgment; and whoso shall say to his brother Raca, shall be in danger of the council. But whosoever shall say, thou fool, shall be in danger of hell fire." For several years my heart was in continual sorrow. And I believe the Almighty beheld from his holy habitation the affliction wherewith I was afflicted, and heard the false misrepresentations wherewith I was misrepresented; and there was none to help. Then I cried unto the Lord in my troubles. And thus for wise and holy purposes best known to himself, he has raised me in the midst of my enemies to vindicate my wrongs before this people, and to reprove them for sin as I have reasoned to them of righteousness and judgment to come. "For as the heavens are higher than the earth, so are his ways above our ways, and his thoughts above our thoughts." I believe, that for wise and holy purposes best known to himself, he hath unloosed my tongue and put his word into my mouth in order to confound and put all those to shame that have rose up against me. For he hath clothed my face with steel and lined my forehead with brass. He hath put his testimony within me and engraven his seal on my forehead. And with these weapons I have indeed set the fiends of earth and hell at defiance.

What if I am a woman; is not the God of ancient times the God of these modern days? Did he not raise up Deborah to be a mother and a judge in Israel? Did not Queen Esther save the lives of the Jews? And Mary Magdalene first declare the resurrection of Christ from the dead? Come, said the woman of Samaria, and see a man that hath told me all things that ever I did; is not this the Christ? St. Paul declared that it was a shame for a woman to speak in public, yet our great High Priest and Advocate did not condem the woman for a more notorious offense than this; neither will he condemn this worthless worm. The bruised reed he will not break, and the smoking flax he will not quench till he send forth judgment unto victory. Did St. Paul but know of our wrongs and deprivations, I presume he would make no objection to our pleading in public for our rights.

Again: Holy women ministered unto Christ and the apostles; and women of refinement in all ages, more or less, have had a voice in moral, religious, and political subjects. Again : Why the Almighty hath imparted unto me the power of speaking thus I cannot tell. "And Jesus lifted up his voice and said, I thank thee, O Father, Lord of heaven and earth, that thou hast hid these things from the wise and prudent and hast revealed them unto babes : even so. Father, for so it seemed good in thy sight.

But to convince you of the high opinion that was formed of the capacity and ability of woman by the ancients, I would refer you to "Sketches of the Fair Sex." Read to the fifty-first page, and you will find that several of the northern nations imagined that women could look into futurity, and that they had about them an inconceivable something approaching to divinity. Perhaps the idea was only the effect of the sagacity common to the sex, and the advantages which their natural address gave them over rough and simple warriors. Perhaps, also, those barbarians, surprised at the influence which beauty has over force, were led to ascribe to the supernatural attraction a charm which they could not comprehend. A belief, however, that the Deity more readily communicates himself to women, has at one time or other prevailed in every quarter of the earth ; not only among the Germans and the Britons, but all the people of Scandinavia were possessed of it. Among the Greeks, women delivered the oracles. The respect the Romans paid to the Sybils is well known. The Jews had their prophetesses. The prediction of the Egyptian women obtained much credit at Rome, even unto the emperors. And in most barbarous nations all things that have the appearance of being supernatural, the mysteries of religion, the secrets of physic, and the rights of magic, were in the possession of women.

If such women as are here described have once existed, be no longer astonished. then, my brethren and friends, that God at this eventful period should raise up your own females to strive by their example, both in public and private, to assist those who are endeavoring to stop the strong current of prejudice that flows so profusely against us at present. No longer ridicule their efforts, it will be counted for sin. For God makes use of feeble means sometimes to bring about his most exalted purposes.

In the fifteenth century, the general spirit of this period is worthy of observation. We might then have seen women preaching and mixing themselves in controversies. Women occupying the chairs of Philosophy and Justice; women haranguing in Latin before the Pope; women writing in Greek and studying in Hebrew; nuns were poetesses and women of quality divines; and young girls who had studied eloquence would, with the sweetest countenances and the most plaintiff voices. pathetically exhort the Pope and the Christian princes to declare war against the Turks. Women in those days devoted their leisure hours to contemplation and study. The religious spirit which has animated women in all ages showed itself at this time. It has made them, by turns, martyrs, apostles, warriors, and concluded in making them divines and scholars.

Why cannot a religious spirit animate us now? Why cannot we become divines and scholars? Although learning is somewhat requisite, yet recollect that those great apostles, Peter and James, were ignorant and unlearned. They were taken from the fishing-boat. and made fishers of men.

In the thirteenth century, a young lady of Bologne devoted herself to the study of the Latin language and of the laws. At the age of twenty-three she pronounced a funeral oration in Latin in the great church of Bologne; and to be admitted as an orator, she had neither need of indulgence on account of her youth or of her sex. At the age of twenty-six she took the degree of doctor of laws, and began publicly to expound the Institutes of Justinian. At the age of thirty, her great reputation raised her to a chair, where she taught the law to a prodigious concourse of scholars from all nations. She joined the charms and accomplishments of a woman to all the knowledge of a man. And such was the power of her eloquence, that her beauty was only admired when her tongue was silent.

What if such women as are here described should rise among our sable race? And it is not impossible; for it is not the color of the skin that makes the man or the woman, but the principle formed in the soul. Brilliant wit will shine, come from whence it will; and genius and talent will not hide the brightness of its lustre.

But to return to my subject, The mighty work of reformation has begun among this people. The dark clouds of ignorance are dispersing. The light of science is bursting forth. Knowledge is beginning to flow; nor will its moral influence be extinguished till its refulgent ray have spread over us from East to West and from North to South. Thus far is this mighty work begun, but not as yet accomplished. Christians must awake from their slumbers. Religion must flourish among them before the church will be built up in its purity or immorality be suppressed.

Yet, notwithstanding your prospects are thus fair and bright, I am about to leave you, perhaps never more to return; for I find it is no use for me, as an individual, to try to make myself useful among my color in this city. It was contempt for my moral and religious opinions in private that drove me thus before a public. Had experience more plainly shown me that it was the nature of man to crush his fellow, I should not have thought it so hard. Wherefore, my respected friends, let us no longer talk of prejudice till prejudice becomes extinct at home. Let us no longer talk of opposition till we cease to oppose our own. For while these evils exist, to talk is like giving breath to the air and labor to the wind, Though wealth is far more highly prized than humble merit, yet none of these things move me. Having God for my friend and portion, what have I to fear? Promotion cometh neither from the East or West; and as long as it is the will of God, I rejoice that I am as I am; for man in his best estate is altogether vanity. Men of eminence have mostly risen from obscurity; nor will I, although a female of a darker hue, and far more obscure than they, bend my head or hang my harp upon willows; for though poor, I will virtuous prove. And if it is the will of my Heavenly Father to reduce me to penury and want, I am ready to say: Amen; even so be it. "The foxes have holes, and the birds of the air have nests, but the Son of man hath not where to lay his head."

During the short period of my Christian warfare, I have indeed had to contend against the fiery darts of the devil. And was it not that the righteous are kept by the mighty power of God through faith unto salvation, long before this I should have proved to be like the seed by the wayside; for it has actually appeared to me, at different periods, as though the powers of earth and hell had combined against me, to prove my overthrow. Yet amidst their dire attempts, I found the Almighty to be "a friend that sticketh closer than a brother." He never will forsake the soul that leans on him; though he chastens and corrects, it is for the soul's best interest. "And as a father pitieth his children, so the Lord pitieth them that fear him."

But some of you said: "Do not talk so much about religion; the people do not wish to hear you. We know these things; tell us something we do not know." If you know these things, my dear friends, and have performed them, far happier and more prosperous would you now have been. "He that knoweth his Lord's will, and obeyeth it not, shall be beaten with many stripes." Sensible of this, I have, regardless of the frowns and scoffs of a guilty world, plead up religion and the pure principles of morality among you. Religion is the most glorious theme that mortals can converse upon. The older it grows the more new beauties it displays. Earth, with its brilliant attractions, appears mean and sordid when compared to it. It is that fountain that has no end, and those that drink thereof shall never thirst; for it is, indeed, a well of water springing up in the soul unto everlasting life.

Again: Those ideas of greatness which are held forth to us are vain delusions—are airy visions which we shall never realize. All that man can say or do can never elevate us; it is a work that must be effected between God and ourselves. And how? By dropping all political discussions in our behalf; for these, in my opinion, sow the seed of discord and strengthen the cord of prejudice. A spirit of animosity is already risen, and unless it is quenched, a fire will burst forth and devour us, and our young will be slain by the sword. It is the sovereign will of God that our condition should be thus and so. "For he hath formed one vessel for honor, and another for dishonor." And shall the clay say to him that formed it: Why hast Thou formed me thus? It is high time for us to drop political discussions; and when our day of deliverance comes, God will provide a way for us to escape, and fight his own battles.

Finally, my brethren, let us follow after godliness, and the things which make for peace. Cultivate your own minds and morals; real merit will elevate you. Pure religion will burst your fetters. Turn your attention to industry. Strive to please your employers. Lay up what you earn. And remember that the grave distinction withers and the high and low are alike renowned.

But I draw to a conclusion. Long will the kind sympathy of some much-loved friend be written on the tablet of my memory, especially those kind individuals who have stood by me like pitying angels and befriended me when in the midst of difficulty, many blessings rest on them. Gratitude is all the tribute I can offer. A rich reward awaits them.

To my unconverted friends, one and all, I would say, shortly this frail tenement of mine will be dissolved and lie mouldering in ruins. O, solemn thought! Yet why should I revolt, for it is the glorious hope of a blessed immortality beyond the grave that has supported me thus far through this vale of tears. Who among you will strive to meet me at the right hand of Christ? For the great day of retribution is fast approaching, and who shall be able to abide his coming? You are forming characters for eternity. As you live, so you will die; as death leaves you, so judgment will find you. Then shall we receive the glorious welcome: "Come, ye blessed of my Father, inherit the kingdom prepared for you from before the foundation of the world." Or hear the heart-rending sentence: "Depart, ye cursed, into everlasting fire prepared for the devil and his angels." When thrice ten thousand years have rolled away, eternity will be but just begun. Your ideas will but just begin to expand. O, eternity, who can unfathom thine end or comprehend thy beginning?

Dearly beloved, I have made myself contemptible in the eyes of many, that I might win some. But it has been like labor in vain. "Paul may plant and Apollos water, but God alone giveth the increase."

To my brethren and sisters in the church I would say, be ye clothed with the breast-plate of righteousness, having your loins girt about you with truth, prepared to meet the bridegroom at his coming; for blessed are those servants that are found watching.

Farewell! In a few short years from now we shall meet in those upper regions where parting will be no more. There we shall sing and shout, and shout and sing, and make heaven's high arches ring. There we shall range in rich pastures and partake of those living streams that never dry. O, blissful thought! Hatred and contentention shall cease, and we shall join with redeemed millions in ascribing glory and honor and riches and power and blessing to the Lamb that was slain and to Him that sitteth upon the throne. Nor eye hath seen nor ear heard, neither hath it entered into the heart of man to conceive of the joys that are prepared for them that love God. Thus far has my life been almost a life of complete disappointment. God has tried me as by fire. Well was I aware that if I contended boldly for his cause I must suffer. Yet I chose rather to suffer affliction with his people than to enjoy the pleasures of sin for a season. And I believe that the glorious declaration was about to be made applicable to me that was made to God's ancient covenant people by the prophet: "Comfort ye, comfort ye, my people; say unto her that her warfare is accomplished. and that her inquities are pardoned. I believe that a rich reward awaits me. if not in this world, in the world to come. O, blessed reflection. The bitterness of my soul has departed from those who endeavored to discourage and hinder me in my Christian progress: and I can now forgive my enemies, bless those who have hated me, and cheerfully pray for those who have despitefully used and persecuted me.

Fare you well! farewell!

MARIA W. STEWART.

NEW YORK, *April* 14, 1834.